I0823035

Praise for *Could President Trump Constitutionally Serve a Third Term?*

"Professor Alan Dershowitz is always thoughtful and frequently provocative, and this book is both. He shows that the Twenty-Second Amendment was clearly meant to prohibit a person from serving three terms as president, but there are ways that this could be circumvented given how it is written. Although it is unlikely to ever happen, Professor Dershowitz shows how important it is to fix this and how easy it would be to do so."

—Erwin Chemerinsky, dean and professor, University of California, Berkeley School of Law

"Either Alan Dershowitz is wrong or naive textualism is absurd. As either disjunct is fun, that's reason enough to read this compelling and beautifully written Hail Mary for the proposition that Donald Trump (and, as he argues, Barack Obama) could serve for a third term."

—Lawrence Lessig, Roy L. Furman Professor of Law and Leadership, Harvard Law School

"Clear-eyed, rigorous, nonpartisan analysis, together with fascinating historical evidence. Required reading for anyone who wants to know what the Constitution actually says about whether Trump could legally serve a third presidential term."

—Jed Rubenfeld, professor of law, Yale Law School

"Most lawyers have shunned even the possibility of making this argument. One called it "unthinkable." Yet here it is, made within the norms of proper constitutional analysis. Of course, those norms allow room for disagreement. And I do disagree. But we all should applaud—and learn from—its principled mastery. And its boldness.

—Richard Parker, Williams Professor of Justice, Harvard Law School

"This timely book is especially essential for readers who share the author's conclusion that a twice-elected president should not remain in office beyond two terms; that conclusion can be most effectively defended based on familiarity with the pertinent constitutional analysis, which the book cogently lays out. Carefully analyzing the text and purposes of the key constitutional provisions, the book evenhandedly spells out the most plausible arguments for and against the constitutional (im)permissibility of a third presidential term. Dispelling widespread public misunderstanding that the Constitution's text clearly bars a third term, the book notes that liberal constitutional scholars have argued that it could permit potential third terms for former Presidents Clinton and Obama. The book well equips opponents of a third Trump term to understand and counter those arguments."

—Nadine Strossen, John Marshall Harlan II Professor of Law Emerita, New York Law School; past national president, American Civil Liberties Union (1991–2008)

Also by Alan Dershowitz

Jewish Blood Is No Longer Cheap
The Preventive State
Trump to Harvard: Go Fund Yourself
Palestinianism
The Ten Big Anti-Israel Lies
War on Woke
War Against the Jews
Get Trump
Dershowitz on Killing
The Price of Principle
The Case for Vaccine Mandates
The Case for Color-Blind Equality in an Age of Identity Politics
The Case Against the New Censorship: Protecting Free Speech from Big Tech, Progressives, and Universities
Cancel Culture: The Latest Attack on Free Speech and Due Process
The Case for Liberalism in an Age of Extremism: or, Why I Left the Left But Can't Join the Right
Confirming Justice—Or Injustice?: A Guide to Judging RGB's Successor
Defending the Constitution
Guilt by Accusation: The Challenge of Proving Innocence in the Age of #MeToo
Defending Israel: The Story of My Relationship with My Most Challenging Client
The Case Against Impeaching Trump
The Case Against BDS: Why Singling Out Israel for Boycott Is Anti-Semitic and Anti-Peace
Trumped Up: How Criminalization of Political Differences Endangers Democracy
Electile Dysfunction: A Guide for Unaroused Voters
The Case Against the Iran Deal
Terror Tunnels: The Case for Israel's Just War Against Hamas
Abraham: The World's First (But Certainly Not Last) Jewish Lawyer
Taking the Stand: My Life in the Law
The Trials of Zion
The Case for Moral Clarity: Israel, Hamas and Gaza
The Case Against Israel's Enemies: Exposing Jimmy Carter and Others Who Stand in the Way of Peace
Is There a Right to Remain Silent? Coercive Interrogation and the Fifth Amendment After 9/11
Finding Jefferson: A Lost Letter, a Remarkable Discovery, and the First Amendment in the Age of Terrorism
Blasphemy: How the Religious Right is Hijacking Our Declaration of Independence
Pre-emption: A Knife That Cuts Both Ways
Rights From Wrongs: A Secular Theory of the Origins of Rights

America on Trial: Inside the Legal Battles That Transformed Our Nation
The Case for Peace: How the Arab-Israeli Conflict Can Be Resolved
The Case for Israel
America Declares Independence
Why Terrorism Works: Understanding the Threat, Responding to the Challenge
Shouting Fire: Civil Liberties in a Turbulent Age
Letters to a Young Lawyer
Supreme Injustice: How the High Court Hijacked Election 2000
Genesis of Justice: Ten Stories of Biblical Injustice that Led to the Ten Commandments and Modern Law
Just Revenge
Sexual McCarthyism: Clinton, Starr, and the Emerging Constitutional Crisis
The Vanishing American Jew: In Search of Jewish Identity for the Next Century
Reasonable Doubts: The Criminal Justice System and the O. J. Simpson Case
The Abuse Excuse: And Other Cop-Outs, Sob Stories, and Evasions of Responsibility
The Advocate's Devil
Contrary to Popular Opinion
Chutzpah
Taking Liberties: A Decade of Hard Cases, Bad Laws, and Bum Raps
Reversal of Fortune: Inside the Von Bülow Case
The Best Defense
Fair and Certain Punishment: Report of the 20th Century Fund Task Force on Criminal Sentencing
Courts of Terror: Soviet Criminal Justice and Jewish Emigration (coauthored with Telford Taylor)
Criminal Law: Theory and Process (with Joseph Goldstein and Richard Schwartz)
Psychoanalysis, Psychiatry, and Law (with Joseph Goldstein and Jay Katz)

Could President Trump Constitutionally Serve a Third Term?

★ ★ ★ ★ ★ ★ ★ ★ ★ ★

My Nonpartisan Legal Analysis

★ ★ ★ ★ ★ ★ ★ ★ ★ ★

Alan Dershowitz

Skyhorse Publishing

Skyhorse Publishing books may be purchased in bulk at special discounts for sales promotion, corporate gifts, fund-raising, or educational purposes. Special editions can also be created to specifications. For details, contact the Special Sales Department, Skyhorse Publishing, 307 Fifth Avenue, 4th Floor, New York, NY 10016 or info@skyhorsepublishing.com.

Regnery® is an imprint of Skyhorse Publishing, Inc.®, a Delaware corporation.

Visit our website at www.skyhorsepublishing.com.
Please follow our publisher Tony Lyons on Instagram @tonylyonsisuncertain.

10 9 8 7 6 5 4 3 2 1

Library of Congress Cataloging-in-Publication Data is available on file.

Cover design by Brian Peterson

Print ISBN: 978-1-5107-8706-3
Ebook ISBN: 978-1-5107-8707-0

Printed in The United States of America

Dedication

This controversial book is dedicated to those who disagree with me, but who agree that all sides should be presented in the marketplace of ideas.

Acknowledgments

I am grateful to those academic colleagues who were willing to read drafts of this manuscript at a time when others condemned the very act of writing it. They include Professors Erwin Chemerinsky, Aaron Voloj Dessauer, Larry Lessig, Richard Parker, Jed Rubenfeld, and Nadine Strossen whose intellectual seriousness, generosity of spirit, and commitment to principled inquiry represent the best traditions of the legal academy. I am also thankful to my friends for their thoughtful comments, encouragement, and support throughout this process. As always, I acknowledge the love and support of Carolyn, who helps me even when she disagrees.

Finally, I thank Hector Carosso and Adam Szetela of Skyhorse Publishing for their careful and perceptive editorial work.

All conclusions, as well as any errors or omissions, are my own.

Contents

From the Author

No one will love this book—except those who appreciate an honest, objective, nonpartisan analysis of a complex series of interesting issues and questions to which there are no definitive resolutions or answers that will satisfy everyone. To the contrary, my research, analysis, and conclusions will annoy and aggravate those seeking certainty in a world of uncertainty.

Preface

My Purpose in Writing This Book

★ ★ ★

The 22nd Amendment, as written, leaves open the possibility that a two-term president could serve a third term, as long as he was not "elected" to that term. This book shows—as a thought experiment, not as a guide to partisan action—how that could happen. It also shows why such a result would be inconsistent with the purpose of that Amendment, and why the only certain way to prevent that possibility in the future is to change its wording by an additional amendment.[1]

Anyone who wants to believe that it is clear beyond dispute that under current law a two-term president can never serve a third term will be as disappointed by this book as anyone who wants to believe that it is clear beyond dispute that he can. The book proves beyond dispute only one conclusion: there are more or less cogent arguments on both sides, which are

1 A definitive Supreme Court decision would go a long way in assuring that a two-term president could never serve a third term, but there is no way for citizens to control the High Court's decision-making or to prevent it from reversing its decision, as it has sometimes done. A constitutional amendment can also be reversed, but that requires an overwhelming popular consensus.

presented as objectively as if I were conducting a law school seminar on these issues. Those are my favorite types of subjects to think and write about. Hence this book.

My aim is to consider constitutional questions without regard to partisan or ideological considerations by examining text, structure, history, and precedent, and by considering how courts are likely to respond.

As Oliver Wendell Holmes once put it, the job of a lawyer is to predict what the courts will do in fact.[2] I try to apply the same interpretive standards regardless of political consequences and let the chips fall where they may. Or in the words of Chief Justice John Roberts, calling balls and strikes.[3] Even umpires have wider or narrower strike zones, but fair ones apply them equally to both sides. No scholar who brings their own experiences and perspectives to their work can rule out the possibility of unconscious or even conscious bias. My conscious biases favor free speech, due process, and equal rights, applied equally to both sides of the partisan divide.

Few issues are more partisan or political today than whether President Donald Trump could or should serve a third term.[4]

---

2 Oliver Wendell Holmes Jr., "The Path of the Law," 10 *Harvard Law Review* 457 (1897). ("The reason why it is a profession, why people pay lawyers to argue for them or to advise them, is that in societies like ours the command of the public force is instrusted to the judges in certain cases, and the whole power of the state will be put forth, if necessary, to carry out their judgments and decrees. . . . The object of our study, then, is prediction, the prediction of the incidence of the public force through the instrumentalities of the courts.")

3 "Confirmation Hearing on the Nomination of John G. Roberts Jr. to be Chief Justice of the United States," Hearings before the Committee on the Judiciary, United States Senate, 109th Congress, U.S. Government Printing Office, 2005, pp 55–56, available at https://www.uscourts.gov/about-federal-courts/educational-resources/supreme-court-landmarks/nomination-process/chief-justice-roberts-statement-nomination-process.

4 President Trump repeatedly flirted with the idea of running for a third term—if not himself then through his surrogates. Trump adviser Stephen Bannon said in a recent interview that Trump is "going to get a third term" and "there

Most Americans have personal views on the subject[5] but I have done my best not to allow those views to determine the constitutional analysis that follows. At the same time, judges and scholars are not immune to the influence of their own perspectives and assumptions, particularly in periods of intense political polarization like ours.

This book advances a simple but uncomfortable and controversial claim: It is currently not clear whether a president can ever serve a third term. The text of the 22nd Amendment bars a person from being *elected* president more than twice, but it does not bar a twice-elected president from *serving* again through non-electoral means, such as succession or appointment. At the same time, the historical record strongly suggests that the amendment's framers intended to prohibit a third term *by whatever means it is achieved.*

If both propositions are correct—and research shows that they are—then courts confront a rare and difficult constitutional dilemma: What should prevail when clear text of an amendment points in one direction and its apparent purpose point in another?

---

is a plan" to achieve this, without specifying what the plan is. (https://nypost.com/2025/10/27/us-news/trump-rules-out-running-as-vances-vp-to-gain-third-term-but-open-to-bannon-plan-let-aoc-go-against-trump/) Trump's son Eric also recently said he cannot rule out a third term. (https://nypost.com/2025/11/05/us-news/eric-trump-refuses-to-rule-out-dad-running-for-third-term-or-himself-while-discussing-2024-victory-on-pod-force-one/%20). John Bolton, Trump's former national security advisor from 2018–2019, said that Trump frequently spoke about a third term and that he would like to do it. Michael Wilner, "A Trump Bid for a Third Term? It Could Get Messy," *Los Angeles Times*, April 1, 2025.

5 In March 2025, I stated in an interview that President Trump would not run for or be elected to a third term, noting that such an outcome would require a constitutional amendment that "could not possibly be enacted in time." That statement did not address the separate constitutional contingencies involving succession or non-electoral service analyzed here. Michael Wilner, "A Trump Bid for a Third Term? It Could Get Messy," *Los Angeles Times*, April 1, 2025.

Consider whether a twice-elected president could constitutionally serve again under the following circumstances (to be elaborated later):

1. being elected or appointed vice president and later succeeding to the presidency;
2. being elected or appointed Speaker of the House and succeeding under the Presidential Succession Act;
3. becoming vice president through appointment under the 25th Amendment and then succeeding;[6]
4. being chosen by the House of Representatives following an Electoral College deadlock.

I do *not* argue that any of these outcomes would be politically wise or desirable—only that the constitutional text may not clearly foreclose them.

The conclusions reached in this book will undoubtedly generate disagreement. The aim of the analysis, however, is neither to persuade nor to provoke, but to examine a disputed constitutional question with as much clarity and rigor as possible. The arguments should be evaluated on their reasoning and evidence, not on their political implications.

I have been urged not to write this book out of fear that my conclusions might lead to political outcomes that are undesirable to many. That consideration, however, has never guided

6 Under Section 2 of the 25th Amendment, upon the vacancy of a vice presidency, the president nominates a replacement who takes office only after being confirmed by a majority vote in both the House and the Senate. Prior to the enactment of the 25th Amendment in 1967, the vice presidency position was vacant sixteen times or a total of thirty-eight years. See "The 25th Amendment: Succession of the Presidency," Feb.10, 2027, available at https://prologue.blogs.archives.gov/2017/02/10/the-25th-amendment-succession-of-the-presidency. This process was used twice in the 1970s: when Spiro Agnew resigned, President Nixon nominated Gerald Ford, and when Ford became president, he nominated Nelson Rockefeller.

my approach to thinking, researching, teaching, or writing about the Constitution.

Some readers will be skeptical of my claim to neutrality because of my professional relationship with President Trump, especially my role as one of his attorneys during his first impeachment. That skepticism is understandable. My answer is methodological rather than rhetorical: the constitutional analysis that follows does not depend on who benefits from it.

This book is not intended to give any candidate "ideas." My legal analysis is the same whether the outcome would benefit Donald Trump, Barack Obama, Bill Clinton, George W. Bush, or any other twice-elected president in the future. Readers should judge the analysis on its reasoning, not on assumptions about my motivations.

Some longtime friends will argue that by writing this book, I am legitimizing President Trump's attempt to defy yet another constitutional taboo. My colleague at Harvard Law School, Professor Noah Feldman, for example, argues that the possibility of a two-term president serving a third term—whether by election or by succession—should be "unthinkable."[7] His position is not merely that such a scenario should be rejected on the merits, but that it is improper even to *consider* or hypothetically analyze whether the 22nd Amendment, as written, might ever permit it, even under extreme contingencies. He worries that exploring the boundaries of the textual prohibition risks normalizing the idea itself.

This attitude is not unique to Professor Feldman. As Professor Deborah Pearlstein of Princeton told *The Washington Post* recently: "Trump is constitutionally ineligible to serve a

---

7 Noah Feldman: "How Constitutional Limits Become Negotiable," Bloomberg Opinion, Nov. 28, 2025.

third term. End of story."[8] Even if not intended that way, the remark has the effect of foreclosing discussion, and it brings to mind the famous Ring Lardner quip, "'Shut up!' he explained."[9]

Telling someone to be quiet, without giving an explanation, is a form of censorship. These scholars are not merely asserting a conclusion; they are insisting that the question itself must not be asked.

Professor Feldman's elaboration makes the point explicit:

> [T]he way to fight back against unthinkable legal ideas is to demonstrate precisely how adopting them would break the broader framework on which constitutional law rests.
>
> Take the idea that Trump could serve a third term by running for vice president and then having the new president resign. This is an unthinkable legal idea because we all understand that the 22nd Amendment prevents anyone from serving more than two terms. The amendment says you can't be elected twice. It also specifies that a vice president who serves more than two years of his predecessor's term can't serve two full terms. Together, these provisions make it unmistakably clear that it would be unconstitutional for Trump to run for vice president and then take over from Vance.
>
> If it were possible to get around this amendment by exploiting the framers' failure to explicitly forbid someone from being elected president twice and then again as vice president, it would tear the fabric of constitutional law in a fundamental way. It would make it fair game to violate almost

---

8 Leo Sands, "Can Trump Run for a Third Term? The 22nd Amendment Flatly Prevents It," *Washington Post*, March 31, 2025.

9 Ring Lardner, *The Young Immigrunts*, p. 78 (1920).

> any constitutional provision through linguistic manipulation. . . .
>
> [T]his kind of literal reading of the Constitution would fundamentally disrupt how the Constitution operates as the body of law. It's clear why the unthinkable should stay unthinkable: Because embracing such ideas would render the entire structure of the law unable to function properly.
>
> Keeping the unthinkable in the category of unthinkable is therefore not a hopeless task, whether in law or in politics. It simply requires deliberate effort to show people how accepting the unthinkable would upend their worldview.[10]

Professor Feldman offers forceful defenses of what he regards as a necessary constitutional taboo, but his argument focuses more on warning about the disruptive consequences of even considering alternative interpretations than on explaining why the constitutional text itself rules them out. This mode of argument is not new, and it has often been invoked in moments of constitutional anxiety.

History offers cautionary examples. Monarchists once criminalized "compassing the death of the king"[11]—that is, merely imagining the king's death—on the theory that entertaining a forbidden thought would normalize it. George Bernard Shaw famously observed that "assassination is the extreme form of censorship"[12]; banning even thinking about it, in that sense, becomes its penultimate form.

---

10 Noah Feldman, "How Constitutional Limits Become Negotiable," Bloomberg Opinion, Nov. 28, 2025.

11 See William Blackstone, "Commentaries on the Laws of England (Book IV, Ch. 6, 'Of High Treason')," available at https://avalon.law.yale.edu/18th_century/blackstone_bk4ch6.asp.

12 George Bernard Shaw, "The Shewing-Up of Blanco Posnet," Elizabeth Knowles (ed.) *Oxford Dictionary of Modern Quotations* (2007) p. 293.

I reject that extreme manifestation of censorship, including the suppression of ideas offered merely as thought experiments. I *am* going to think about it, analyze it, and debate it on its merits and demerits. We are not dealing with a matter of objective disprovable fact—such as Holocaust denial or whether Elvis is alive—where reasonable debate is foreclosed. We are dealing with a contested question of constitutional interpretation.

The reaction to the mere suggestion that the question of whether a twice-elected president can serve a third term is worth analyzing confirms just how powerful that taboo has become. After the *Wall Street Journal* ran an article about this book's forthcoming publication in December 2025, it sparked a predictable backlash.[13] Professor Richard W. Painter tweeted: "This is just plain stupid. The 22nd Amendment is written in plain English. No third term."[14] In other words, "'Shut up!' he explained."

Others have likewise accused me of advising—or advocating for—President Trump to seek a third term. Anyone reading this book carefully cannot reasonably conclude that it is partisan advocacy rather than a neutral exercise in constitutional analysis. Former President Barack Obama, because of his relative youth (sixty-four), is at least as likely to benefit from my analysis as seventy-nine-year-old President Trump.

Despite what some critics may argue, this book does not advocate for President Trump—or anyone else—to serve a third term. Outside of highly improbable, though not impossible, hypotheticals, it is difficult to imagine likely circumstances in which it would be wise for a twice-elected president to remain in office beyond two terms.

---

13 Brian Schwartz, "Trump Told By Alan Dershowitz Constitutionality of Third Term is Unclear," *Wall Street Journal*, Dec. 17, 2025.

14 Tweet from Dec. 18, 2025 https://x.com/RWPUSA.

But rejecting that outcome does not require pretending that the Constitution clearly resolves the issue, when it clearly does not. Even critics quoted by the *Wall Street Journal* implicitly conceded the point. Hofstra Law Professor James Sample dismissed my argument as "absurd," yet acknowledged that a former twice-elected president could, at least in theory, serve a third term if he returned to the presidency through non-elective means—such as becoming Speaker of the House and later assuming the presidency through succession rather than election.[15] Far from being "unthinkable," my former Harvard colleague Larry Tribe—the most frequently cited constitutional law scholar of our time and a long-standing critic of President Trump—has acknowledged that neither the 22nd nor the 12th Amendment renders Trump constitutionally ineligible to serve a third term, so long as he is not elected to it.[16]

Even Kathleen Sullivan, the former Stanford Law School dean and coauthor of Professor Feldman's constitutional law casebook,[17] has concurred with this assessment, stating that under her reading of the 22nd Amendment a twice-elected president could, under certain circumstances, serve a third term through succession or other non-electoral means.[18]

---

15 Brian Schwartz, "Trump Told by Alan Dershowitz Constitutionality of Third Term Is Unclear," *Wall Street Journal*, Dec. 17, 2025.

16 Tribe tweeted on March 31, 2025 "Anyone discounting a 3d Trump term per the 22d am + the 12th am is thinking magically," Tribe wrote on X (formerly Twitter), referencing the 22nd and 12th amendments to the U.S. Constitution. I discuss Tribe's views on p. 58.

17 Noah R. Feldman and Kathleen M. Sullivan, *Constitutional Law* (22nd Ed., Foundation Press 2025).

18 In 2016, amid speculation that presidential candidate Hillary Clinton might select her husband, the twice-elected former president Bill Clinton, as her running mate, Sullivan observed that "as I read it [the 22nd Amendment] does not preclude a Clinton-Clinton ticket.... Bill, if elected VP, could become president in the event that President Hillary became incapacitated; he just could not run for reelection from that successor post." Quoted in Peter Baker, "VP Bill? It Depends on the Meaning of 'Elected,'" *The Washington*

These concessions underscore the very point this book makes: the constitutional text is far less determinate than is commonly assumed. The "plain English" of the 22nd Amendment may permit a twice-elected President to serve a third term if not elected to it, even though—as will become clear—the Amendment's evident purpose points in the opposite direction.

Even Professor Feldman acknowledges that "once in a while . . . an initially unthinkable idea gains traction," especially when prestigious lawyers with cultural capital engage with arguments once dismissed as "off-the-wall."[19]

We cannot know in advance which arguments will move from the margins to the mainstream.[20] But if a legitimate constitutional issue presents itself—one in which the text, structure, and history allow for reasonable debate—it deserves serious, good-faith analysis rather than preemptive denunciation. In that spirit, I challenge any former colleague to address my unthinkable arguments in the marketplace of ideas, either in an open debate or a written exchange.

Moreover, treating a subject as taboo often backfires. As I have learned from co-teaching a course on taboos with my friend and colleague Steven Pinker, enforced silence creates a vacuum. When responsible voices self-censor, the resulting space is too often filled by those whose reasoning is driven by

---

Post, Oct. 19, 2016.

19 Noah Feldman, "How Constitutional Limits Become Negotiable," Bloomberg Opinion, Nov. 28, 2025.

20 As John Stuart Mill put it in his famous critique of censoring ideas, "The peculiar evil of silencing the expression of an opinion is, that it is robbing the human race. . . . If the opinion is right, they are deprived of the opportunity of exchanging error for truth; if wrong, they lose . . . what is almost as great a benefit, the clearer perception and livelier impression of truth, produced by its collision with error." John Stuart Mills, *Liberty* (London: Longmans, Greer, Reader and Dyer, 1869).

desired outcomes rather than principled method—whether on the left or the right. As will be discussed, few commentators raised 22nd Amendment objections when liberal scholars floated the idea of Bill Clinton running for vice president in 2000 with Vice President Al Gore as presidential candidate.[21] My aim is to call the question straight, without regard to whose political ox is gored (excuse the pun).

Some have asked—including respected colleagues—why not wait until after the next election to publish this analysis, thus not opening myself to the charge that I am trying to influence current events. My answer is that it is better to address such issues in the abstract, before partisans take sides about specific presidents without regard to the merits or demerits of the constitutional arguments. The moment for nonpartisan dispassionate analysis is now. Once partisan passions are inflamed, the opportunity for principled and nuanced reasoning will sharply diminish. Objectivity is often the first casualty of partisanship.

The crucial point is that a question as seemingly basic as whether a twice-elected president may serve again under certain circumstances is not definitely settled. Any scholar who asserts otherwise is not engaging the issue with intellectual rigor—or as Professor Tribe put it, is guilty of "magical thinking."[22] Such certainty often reflects political preference rather than objective legal analysis.

Having taught law for over fifty years, I believe it is essential to provide citizens with nuanced analyses of difficult and controversial constitutional issues. This commitment has

21 See e.g., Michael C. Dorf, "The Case for a Gore-Clinton Ticket," Findlaw, July 31, 2000, available at https://supreme.findlaw.com/legal-commentary/the-case-for-a-gore-clinton-ticket.htm; Thomas L. Friedman, "A Modest Proposal," *New York Times*, July 7, 2000.

22 Tweet from March 31, 2025.

guided not only my academic work but also my public writing, media appearances, podcast, and broader efforts as a public intellectual.

So read this short book with the same openness of mind with which I have tried to write it.

Introduction

The "Plain English" of the 22nd Amendment

★ ★ ★

Most Americans (and most legal scholars) believe that the plain English of the 22nd Amendment categorically prohibits a two-term president from *serving* a third term. After all, it was enacted in direct response to President Franklin Delano Roosevelt being elected four times, (he died just weeks into his fourth term). It was also enacted in response to the leaders on both sides of the Second World War who were serving long, sometimes indefinite terms. Its purpose was to prohibit such enduring leadership. Here is the text of Article 1 of the 22nd Amendment. Read it carefully because much of what follows is based on this text:

> No person shall be *elected* to the office of the President more than twice, and no person who has <u>held</u> the office of President, or *acted* as President, for more than two years of a term to which some other person was *elected* President shall be *elected* to the office of the President more than once.

> But this Article shall not apply to any person *holding* the office of President when this Article was proposed by the Congress, and shall not prevent any person who may be *holding* the office of President, or *acting* as President, during the term within which this Article becomes operative from *holding* the office of President or *acting* as President during the remainder of such term. (emphases added)

Notice that the text distinguished concepts: "elected," "held," or "holding" and "acting" or "acted." Even a causal reading shows that the text of this amendment provides a loophole bigger than the newly expanded White House. There is nothing in its provisions that expressly exclude a president who has been elected twice from <u>serving</u> a third term—as long as he is not <u>elected</u> a third time. "No personal shall be elected . . ."

In other words, if a president who has served two terms <u>ascends</u> to the presidency in a manner <u>other than by election</u>, the text does not explicitly disqualify him from serving. Consider the following three hypotheticals:

Hypothetical 1. A president who has completed his two elected terms could be chosen as vice president. (There are a number of ways in which a person could become vice president, other than being elected.) If the president were to resign, die or be removed via impeachment or the 25th Amendment, could this vice president then become president since he would have ascended to the presidency by means other than through an election? The issue is not merely hypothetical. It was debated in the 2016 election when Hillary Clinton was asked whether she would consider choosing her husband, twice-elected Bill Clinton, to be vice president.[23] And the idea has been floated

23 Tom LoBianco, "Hillary Clinton: Bill as VP Has 'Crossed Her Mind,'" CNN Sept. 15, 2015.

now by Trump Advisor Steve Bannon, who has suggested that Trump could serve a third term if Vice President JD Vance and Trump swapped places on the 2028 ticket only to switch back after winning.[24]

Hypothetical 2. A president who has completed his two elected terms is then chosen to become Speaker of the House.[25] Under current law, the Speaker need not be an elected congressman. If he then becomes president upon the death, resignation or impeachment of the elected president and vice president, may he serve an entire third term? The Speaker of the House could easily have become president following the resignations of both Vice President Spiro Agnew and President Richard Nixon, but for the selection of then Congressman Gerald Ford to become vice president in the interim between these resignations. Without a vice president, Speaker Carl Albert would have ascended to the presidency under the terms of the Constitution and governing law.[26] The same issue would be presented if the former president were serving as secretary of state or any other cabinet position in the statutory line of succession.

---

24 Steven Nelson, "Trump Rules Out Running as Vance's VP to Gain Third Term, but Open to Bannon Plan: 'Let AOC Go Against Trump," *New York Post*, Oct 27, 2025, https://nypost.com/2025/10/27/us-news/trump-rules-out-running-as-vances-vp-to-gain-third-term-but-open-to-bannon-plan-let-aoc-go-against-trump/.

25 With increased life expectancy and longer post-presidential careers, it is entirely conceivable that a former president might later seek and serve in the House of Representatives. This would not be entirely unprecedented. Former president John Quincy Adams, after losing his bid for a second presidential term, went on to serve nine consecutive terms in Congress, becoming one of the most consequential former presidents in legislative history.

26 Carl Albert, "Watergate-Era House Speaker, Dies at 91," *LA Times*, Feb. 6, 2000. ("Twice during his six years as House speaker, Albert stood next in line for the presidency when the nation had no vice president—once after Spiro T. Agnew's resignation from the office in 1973 and again after Gerald R. Ford replaced Richard M. Nixon as president in 1974.").

In this age of mass terrorism, the nation must be prepared for an attack that kills several in the line of succession. Such consideration has been given to the possibility by the creation of the role of "designated survivor," a cabinet member who is isolated from others during events such as the State of the Union address.[27] This scenario has been played out in fictional accounts,[28] but thankfully never in reality.

Hypothetical 3. Another less likely, but constitutionally possible scenario is the following: A two-term president runs for a third term against two other candidates—nothing in the Constitution expressly prohibits a two-term president from *running*, even though he cannot be "elected." There is no majority of electors for any candidate, as there wasn't in the 1800 and several subsequent presidential elections. The House of Representatives must then "choose"—not elect—the president, from the top three "on the list of those voted for as president." The House chooses, not elects, him as president.

Other, even less likely, scenarios have been suggested by constitutional scholars and writers.[29]

Would the Supreme Court sustain—or tolerate by inaction—any such efforts to have a two-term president serve a third term to which he was not "elected"? No one can know with any certainty. (I address this question later on.)

---

27 This practice started during the Cold War in the late 1950s, but the federal government did not publicly acknowledge it by name until 1981. See e.g., "Why Is There A Designated Survivor for the State of the Union Address," National Constitution Center, February 6, 2019, available at https://constitutioncenter.org/blog/why-is-there-a-designated-survivor-for-the-state-of-the-union For a scholarly treatment, see Richard Albert, "The Constitutional Politics of Presidential Succession," 39 *Hofstra L. Rev.* 497, 538 (2011).

28 For example, in the ABC/ Netflix show *Designated Survivor* (2016–2019).

29 Bruce G. Peabody & Scott E. Gant, "The Twice and Future President: Constitutional Interstices and the Twenty-Second Amendment," 83 *Minn. L. Rev.* 565, 568–69 (1999).

The drafters of the 22nd Amendment could easily have precluded all such possibilities, by simply substituting "serve," "hold," or "run" for "elected," thus explicitly prohibiting a two-term president from becoming a third-term president by any means short of amending the Constitution. Though difficult, it is even now possible to correct this opening—loophole—by amending the 22nd Amendment to reflect its apparent purpose.

This choice of words was not inadvertent since the text itself distinguishes between being elected to and "holding" the presidency or "acting" as president. Congress rejected broader terms that would have absolutely precluded a third term. Instead, it provides that a person who has held the presidency or acted as president for more than two years of a second term may not be *elected* to a third term. Moreover, earlier drafts of the amendment would have expressly precluded a two-term president from serving a third time. These drafts were rejected by Congress.[30]

The words enacted by Congress and ratified by the states do not thus expressly preclude a president who has been *elected* to two terms from *holding* that office or *serving* or *acting* as president for a third term, if he or she is not elected to that office.

Some call this a word game, the kind of hairsplitting that gives lawyers and legal scholars a bad name. As the opinion columnist of the *New York Times* Jamelle Bouie recently wrote:

> This [argument] sounds plausible, but it is wrong. First, it treats the Constitution as a language game whose meaning depends less on the text, structure, history and purpose of the document and more on whether you can use the fundamental indeterminacy of language to brute-force your preferred outcome.

---

30 See discussion *infra*, at p. 75.

> But that is not how you should read the Constitution, which isn't a rigid set of instructions to be gamed by clever lawyers, but a political document meant to structure the rules of self-government in the United States. The 22nd Amendment was written to change one of those rules and limit the president's term of office, regardless of the circumstances. Any apparent "loophole" is a mirage produced by a basic misunderstanding of what it is that the Constitution set out to accomplish. A quick look at the history and debate behind the amendment makes this clear.[31]

This critique reflects an understandable impulse, but it misconceives the nature of constitutional interpretation. The constitution is a document of words, whose intentions are not always easy to discern. I'm reminded of the cartoon (reprinted on the back cover of the book) that shows one Founding Father saying to the others: "Just for fun, let's make what is and isn't constitutional kind of wishy-washy." Well, the 22nd Amendment is kind of wishy-washy! Clarity should be expected of constitutional provisions that set out specific qualifications and disqualifications for high office. This is also true of amendments that must be ratified by the legislatures of three-fourths of the states. That is why the actual text matters so much, even more so when it appears in the Constitution, as contrasted with ordinary statutes. A fair reading from the text of the 22nd Amendment alone would seem to suggest that a two-term president can serve, act, or hold office as president for a third term, as long as he is not elected. Whether or not one ultimately agrees with that conclusion, it is not a parlor trick or "language game" to engage with the Constitution's actual words. What

---

31 Jamelle Bouie, "A Third Trump Term Is Not the Charm," *New York Times*, Nov. 1, 2025.

is literally, in Professor Tribe's words, "magical thinking" is to make words that were ratified miraculously disappear or mysteriously change into words that were explicitly rejected.

To be sure, we do not always read constitutional provisions in a relentlessly literal way. Consider the First Amendment. Its text forbids *Congress* from abridging freedom of speech or prohibiting the free exercise of religion, yet we do not infer from that phrasing that the *President* may abridge freedom of speech or prohibit the free exercise of religion. The textual "loophole" is obvious, but we decline to exploit it. When it comes to the great rights protected by the Bill of Rights, we generally resist reading the Constitution as a catalogue of technical gaps to be manipulated.

That instinct, however, does not resolve the present question. This is not simply a dispute between two modes of constitutional interpretation. There is a plausible distinction between provisions that secure fundamental individual rights, as in the Bill of Rights, which we often interpret nonliterally, and provisions that establish electoral rules and qualifications for office, which are technical by design and which we traditionally read with far greater precision.[32]

No one would read the age requirements nonliterally regardless of circumstances. So why should one read the prohibition against a president being "elected more than twice" nonliterally, so as to prohibit serving even if not elected? Perhaps there are good reasons, but surely the burden of persuasion should be on those who ignore or change the literal text.

As the historical record shows, the drafters of the 22nd Amendment understood the difference between being *elected* to the presidency and *serving* as president, and they consciously chose the former while rejecting the latter. Engaging seriously

32 I thank Jed Rubenfeld for this important point.

with that choice is not a language game; it is what fidelity to constitutional text requires—whether or not one ultimately agrees with the conclusion it supports.

Why then did the drafters of the 22nd Amendment make a choice of words that leaves open possibilities of a third term, however unlikely, remote or hypothetical? The evidence suggests that the framers—however defined—of the 22nd Amendment almost certainly intended to preclude a third term, regardless of the mechanism by which it is achieved. That was the purpose of amending the Constitution following the election of FDR to an unprecedented fourth term. That is also what the general public believed was the purpose and intended effect of this amendment.

The academic consensus favors considering such intent and purpose *over* the text. I will explore that consensus and put it in the context of the broader conflict among different modes of constitutional analysis, as I did in my previous books, *Is There a Right To Remain Silent?*, *The Preventive State*, and *Supreme Injustice*.[33] I will then offer my own *constitutional*—not *partisan*—conclusions about whether Donald Trump, or any other two-term president can, not should, serve a third term.

---

33 Alan M. Dershowitz, *Is There a Right to Remain Silent?: Coercive Interrogation and the Fifth Amendment After 9/11* (2006); Alan M. Dershowitz, *The Preventive State: The Challenge of Preventing Serious Harms While Preserving Essential Liberties* (2025) and Alan M. Dershowitz, *Supreme Injustice: How the High Court Hijacked Election 2000* (2001).

PART I

THE HISTORY OF PRESIDENTIAL TERM LIMITS

★ ★ ★

This first part of the book provides a concise historical account of the developments that ultimately led to the adoption of the 22nd Amendment. It begins with the Constitutional Convention, where the Framers opted against formal limits on presidential tenure, believing that decisions regarding duration in office should be determined through the democratic process rather than through constitutional mandate. It then examines how, starting with George Washington and Thomas Jefferson, an informal constitutional norm emerged that limited the presidency to two terms—a practice that generally remained intact for nearly 150 years. Finally, it turns to the administration of Franklin D. Roosevelt, whose presidency not only expanded the power of the office through the New Deal but also overturned the two-term tradition, thereby precipitating the drafting and eventual ratification of the 22nd Amendment.[34]

34 Portions of Part I draw on existing law review literature and secondary historical scholarship rather than independent archival research. These include Bruce Peabody & Scott Gant, "The Twice and Future President," 83 *Minn. L. Rev.* 565 (1999); James Randolph Peck, "Restoring the Balance of Power: Impeachment and the Twenty-Second Amendment," 8 *William & Mary Bill of Rights Journal* 759 (2000); and Thomas H. Neale, "Presidential Terms and Tenure: Perspectives and Proposals for Change," Congressional Research Service, Oct. 19, 2009.

Chapter 1

The Constitutional Convention and *The Federalist Papers*

★ ★ ★

The question of presidential tenure was one of the most difficult structural issues the Constitutional Convention faced in the summer of 1787. There was no previous American experience that provided a useful model other than the governorships of the colonies. Nor were there relevant British precedents.

Under the Articles of Confederation, there was no separate executive branch. Colonial governors often served as agents of the Crown rather than as elected representatives. European monarchies likewise offered little guidance for designing a republic with an independent executive subject to limited tenure. The framers were operating on uncharted constitutional ground, and the stakes were considerable: how to structure an office that was strong enough to govern effectively but sufficiently constrained to prevent despotism.

Following independence from Britain in 1776, most of the colonies preferred weak executives and dominant legislatures.

Their state constitutions largely reflected this view. Several provided for short executive terms, and some barred reelection entirely.

During the Convention, the length of presidential tenure and the question of re-eligibility were vigorously contested. A number of delegates endorsed a single, lengthy, and nonrenewable term, including Edmund Randolph and George Mason of Virginia. Mason worried that unlimited re-eligibility posed the risk of hereditary-style authority, cautioning that without constraints, the presidency might evolve into an "elective Monarchy."[35]

James Madison's *Notes of Debates in the Federal Convention of 1787* record Randolph's and Mason's concerns that continuous re-eligibility would "inspire unconstitutional endeavours to perpetuate himself"[36] in office, pushing the United States perilously close to "a more dangerous monarchy, an elective one."[37] Charles Pinckney of South Carolina echoed these fears, warning that an ambitious executive, if indefinitely re-eligible, could consolidate power over Congress and the populace, ultimately turning the government "into a monarchy, of the worst kind, to wit an elective one."[38]

---

35 George Mason Speech: Virginia Convention, June 17, 1788, in: John P. Kaminski et al., eds., *The Documentary History of the Ratification of the Constitution*, Vol. X: Virginia [3] (Madison, Wis.: Wisconsin Historical Society Press, 1993), 1365–66, available at https://csac.history.wisc.edu/wp-content/uploads/sites/281/2024/04/DC3-04-09-04_Mason-Speech_17Jun88.pdf.

36 Madison Debates, July 19, 1787 (Mr. Randolph), available at https://avalon.law.yale.edu/18th_century/debates_719.asp.

37 Madison Debates, June 4, 1787 (Col. Mason), available at https://avalon.law.yale.edu/18th_century/debates_604.asp.

38 Quoted in James Randolph Peck, "Restoring the Balance of Power: Impeachment and the Twenty-Second Amendment," 8 *William & Mary Bill of Rights Journal* 759, 769 n.48 (2000), available at https://scholarship.law.wm.edu/cgi/viewcontent.cgi?article=1392&context=wmborj.

Initially, the Convention approved a system in which Congress would appoint the president for a seven-year term, without eligibility for reelection.[39]

Other delegates, such as Gouverneur Morris and Alexander Hamilton, opposed such limitations. Morris argued that without the possibility of reelection, Presidents might lose the drive for "public esteem" and "love of fame . . . the great spring to noble and illustrious action."[40] He also feared that prohibiting re-eligibility would encourage corrupt behavior, as presidents might be tempted to "accumulate wealth and provide for his friends."[41]

Ultimately, the Convention settled on a compromise: a four-year term, renewable without limit. This solution reflected both democratic optimism and political pragmatism. A shorter term promoted accountability, while re-eligibility preserved flexibility. By adopting this structure, the Framers left the determination of presidential tenure to political judgment rather than constitutional command.

After the Convention concluded, delegates from New York, North Carolina, and Virginia proposed an amendment restricting any president to no more than two terms. Hamilton responded in *The Federalist Papers*, which sought to persuade the people of New York to ratify the Constitution. In Federalist No. 69, Hamilton argued that the Constitution envisions a re-electable executive, protected by democratic checks against tyranny. The president, he explained, "is to be elected for years;

---

39 Article X Sect. 1 of the August 6, 1787 draft version of the Constitution (stating that the president "shall hold his office during the term of seven years; but shall not be elected a second time."), available at https://www.gilderlehrman.org/sites/default/files/inline-pdfs/00819.01_FPS.pdf.

40 Quoted in Bruce G. Peabody and Scott E. Gant, "The Twice and Future President: Constitutional Interstices and the Twenty-Second Amendment," 83 *Minnesota Law Review*, 565, 572 (1999) *supra* n. 29.

41 *Id.*

and is to re-eligible as often as the people of the United States shall think him worthy of their confidence."[42]

In Federalist No. 72, Hamilton elaborated further on the dangers of limiting eligibility. Echoing Morris's reasoning, he warned that enforcing term limits would undermine "inducements to good behavior" and deter qualified individuals—as only certain men were eligible at the time—from pursuing public service.[43] He also argued that shorter tenure would increase the risk of corruption and abuse of power.[44] Finally, Hamilton emphasized the advantages of retaining proven leadership during critical periods, cautioning that to exclude a capable leader merely because he had previously served would deprive the nation of "the advantage of the experience gained by the chief magistrate in the exercise of office."[45]

Ultimately, Hamilton's and Morris's arguments won the day, and the Constitution was ratified without imposing limits on presidential service. The Framers' confidence in this framework rested in large part on widespread expectations that George Washington would serve as the first president. Ironically, it was not assumed that Washington would voluntarily serve only a few terms, making formal limitations unnecessary; rather, the prevailing expectation was the opposite. Provisions were left open to enable Washington to serve indefinitely if he chose.

---

42 *Federalist Papers*: No. 69, "The Real Character of the Executive," available at https://avalon.law.yale.edu/18th_century/fed69.asp.

43 *Federalist Papers*: No. 72, "The Same Subject Continued, and Re-Eligibility of the Executive Considered" available at https://avalon.law.yale.edu/18th_century/fed72.asp.

44 *Id.* ("An avaricious man, who might happen to fill the office, looking forward to a time when he must at all events yield up the emoluments he enjoyed, would feel a propensity, not easy to be resisted by such a man, to make the best use of the opportunity he enjoyed while it lasted, and might not scruple to have recourse to the most corrupt expedients to make the harvest as abundant as it was transitory.")

45 *Id.*

As constitutional scholar Edward Corwin noted, "the prevailing sentiment of the Convention of 1787 favored the indefinite re-eligibility of the president, a sentiment which was owing in considerable part to the universal expectation that Washington would be the first person to be chosen president, and would be willing to serve indefinitely."[46]

---

46 Edward S. Corwin, *The President: Office and Powers*, 43 (1948) quoted in Peabody & Gant, *supra* n. 26 at 575. (own emphasis)

Chapter 2

Washington, Jefferson, and the Emergence of the Two-Term Tradition

★ ★ ★

The Framers' confidence in Washington proved well-founded. By voluntarily stepping down after two terms in 1796, Washington established an unwritten norm that would shape the presidency for nearly 150 years. The significance of his action may have been as important as any additional clause in Article II of the Constitution.

Nevertheless, while the tradition of a two-term presidency traces its origins to Washington, he was not personally opposed to presidential re-eligibility. In the farewell address (drafted by James Madison) in 1792 and intended for delivery after his first term, Washington endorsed "rotation in office" as aligning "with the spirit of our Constitution,"[47] but that address was never given because Washington chose to run again. In the

47 "Enclosure: Madison's Draft of the Farewell Address," June 20, 1792, available at https://founders.archives.gov/documents/Washington/05-10-02-0318-0002.

1796 Farewell Address (drafted by Alexander Hamilton), the references to "rotation in office" were omitted.

Moreover, one year after presiding over the Convention that rejected term limits, Washington wrote to the Marquis de Lafayette, stating, "on the eligibility of the same person for president, after he should have served a certain course of years. . . . I confess I differ widely myself from Mr. Jefferson and you, as to the necessity or expediency of rotation in that department. The matter was freely discussed in the convention and to my full conviction. . . . I can see no propriety in precluding ourselves from the services of any man who in some great emergency shall be deemed universally most capable of serving the public."[48]

In his farewell address, Washington did not offer a principled reason for his decision to step down from the presidency, instead citing his advanced age and desire for retirement, noting that "every day the encreasing weight of years admonishes me more and more, that the shade of retirement is as necessary to me as it will be welcome."[49]

Whether it was a matter of principle or the longing for "the shade of retirement" the fact remains that Washington did not cling to power. By stepping down, attending the inauguration of his political opponent John Adams, and returning to his

48 "Letter from George Washington to the Marquis de Lafayette," (Apr. 28, 1788), cited in Peabody & Gant, at 557.

49 George Washington, "Farewell Address," 1796, available at https://www.mountvernon.org/george-washington/the-first-president/the-farewell-address. See also Sidney M. Milkis and Michael Nelson, *The American Presidency, Origins and Development*, 1776-2018 (8th ed.), p. 384 (2019) (Washington had stepped down voluntarily from the presidency after two terms "not as a matter of principle, but because he thought the country needed to learn that the Constitution would work even if he were not president. More personally, he longed for the 'shade of retirement.'").

private life, Washington marked the first peaceful transfer of power—now a hallmark of American democracy.

Over time, Washington's *actions*—rather than his *intentions*—came to represent a principled precedent and unwritten constitutional norm.

Thomas Jefferson, the second president to serve two full terms, consistently advocated "rotation in office." Even before his presidency, Jefferson expressed concerns about "perpetual eligibility."[50] In a letter sent from Paris to George Washington before the Constitution was ratified, Jefferson warned that "perpetual eligibility . . . will make [the presidency] for life first, and then hereditary." He continued:

> I was much an enemy to monarchy before I came to Europe. I am ten thousand times more so since I have seen what they are. There is scarcely an evil known in these countries which may not be traced to their king as its source, nor a good which is not derived from the small fibres of republicanism existing among them. I can further say with safety there is not a crowned head in Europe whose talents or merit would entitle him to be elected a vestryman by the people of any parish in America. However I shall hope that before there is danger of this change taking place in the office of President, the good sense and free spirit of our countrymen will make the changes necessary to prevent it.[51]

Jefferson did not abandon these views once he became president and was urged to run for a third term. True to his principles, he offered a steadfast refusal:

---

50 "Thomas Jefferson to George Washington," May 2, 1788, available at https://founders.archives.gov/documents/Jefferson/01-13-02-0059.

51 *Id.*

> If some termination to the services of the Chief Magistrate be not fixed by the Constitution, or supplied by practice, his office, nominally four years, will in fact become for life, and history shows how easily that degenerates into an inheritance. Believing that a representative Government responsible at short periods is that which produces the greatest sum of happiness to mankind, I feel it a duty to do no act which shall essentially impair that principle, and I should unwillingly be the person who, disregarding the sound precedent set by an illustrious predecessor [George Washington], should furnish the first example of prolongation beyond the second term of office.[52]

Jefferson nonetheless recognized a possible exception to this principle. In a letter to John Taylor, he wrote, "There is . . . one circumstance which could engage my acquiescence in another election; to wit, such a division about a successor, as might bring in a monarchist."[53]

After Jefferson stepped down in 1809, the two-term tradition took firm hold. James Madison, James Monroe, Andrew Jackson, and later Woodrow Wilson all completed two terms and declined a third, reinforcing what had become an unwritten

---

52 Thomas Jefferson made a similar point in a letter to John Taylor, an early Senator of Virginia, dated Jan. 6, 1805. Presciently, he even envisioned a constitutional amendment to formalize the precedent set by Washington. Jefferson writes, "I determined to withdraw at the end of my second term. The danger is that the indulgence & attachments of the people will keep a man in the chair after he becomes a dotard, that reelection through life shall become habitual, & election for life follow that. Genl. Washington set the example of voluntary retirement after 8 years. I shall follow it, and a few more precedents will oppose the obstacle of habit to anyone after a while who shall endeavor to extend his term. Perhaps it may beget a disposition to establish it by an amendment of the constitution." Available at https://tile.loc.gov/storage-services/service/mss/mtj/mtj1/032//032_0169_0169.pdf.

53 *Id.*

constitutional norm.[54] As presidential historian Doris Kearns Goodwin noted, "[e]ver since George Washington refused a third term, no man had even tried to achieve the office of the Presidency more than twice."[55]

That statement is somewhat overstated. Some presidents *did* try to achieve a third a term but were unsuccessful. Ulysses S. Grant, who served from 1869 to 1877, sought the 1880 Republican nomination and led for several ballots before losing to James A. Garfield. The tradition remained intact, though not for lack of ambition.

Theodore "Teddy" Roosevelt was another exception. Roosevelt, who served most of McKinley's second term after he was assassinated, was elected president in his own right in 1904. On the night of his election triumph, he declared his adherence to the tradition:

> [o]n the 4th of March next I shall have served three and a half years and this . . . constitutes my first term. The wise caution which limits the President to two terms regards the substance and not the form; and under no circumstances will I be a candidate or accept another nomination.[56]

Roosevelt initially honored this, retiring in 1908. Dissatisfaction with his successor William Howard Taft led him to run again in 1912, explaining that in 1904 he had meant only that he would

---

54 Abraham Lincoln and William McKinley were also elected for a second term, but both were assassinated during their second term in office.

55 Doris Kearns Goodwin, *No Ordinary Time: Franklin & Eleanor Roosevelt: The Home Front in World War II*, 106 (2008).

56 Reported in *The New York Tribune*, Nov. 9, 1904, quoted in Thomas H. Neale, "Presidential Terms and Tenure: Perspectives and Proposals for Change," Congressional Research Service, Oct. 19, 2009, p. 17.

not seek a third *consecutive* term.[57] Denied the Republican nomination, Roosevelt ran as the Progressive Party (Bull Moose Party) candidate, splitting the Republican vote and handing the election to Democrat Woodrow Wilson—the last two-term president prior to FDR.

Despite the efforts by Grant and Roosevelt, the two-term norm held firm for more than a century, confirming its status as an informal constitutional constraint. As historian David Kyvig observed, the idea that a President should not serve beyond two terms was "established by George Washington, reinforced by Thomas Jefferson, and observed for one reason or another by the seven other once-reelected chief executives" up to Franklin D. Roosevelt.[58]

Franklin Delano Roosevelt

For nearly 150 years, the two-term precedent helped anchor American constitutional order. It endured through war, reconstruction, industrial development, and major shifts in national power.

Yet it collapsed under the extraordinary presidency of Franklin Delano Roosevelt, whose tenure transformed both the office and the nation. The only president to serve more than two full terms, Roosevelt was elected in 1932 and took office in 1933 at the height of the Great Depression. Amid mass unemployment and systemic failures, his New Deal policies dramatically expanded the role of the federal government—especially the executive branch.

While popular by 1936, Roosevelt still publicly acknowledged the weight of tradition. In 1937, he declared that it was

57 *Id.* at p. 17.

58 David Kyvig, *Explicit and Authentic Acts: Amending the U.S. Constitution, 1776-1995*, p. 325 (1996).

his "'great ambition . . . [to] turn over this desk and chair in the White House' on Inauguration Day."[59] But in 1940, with Europe engulfed by war and Britain standing nearly alone, he accepted the Democratic nomination for a third term. His justification emphasized global instability and the need for continuity. In his final speech of the 1940 campaign, Roosevelt said: "There is a great storm raging now, that makes things harder for the world. And that storm, which did not start in this land of ours, is the true reason that I would like to stick by these people of ours until we reach the clear, sure footing ahead."[60] In 1944, with World War II ongoing, but close to ending victoriously, he ran and won a fourth term. Though his health had visibly deteriorated, voters still preferred continuity. He died in April 1945, at age sixty-three, shortly after beginning that final term.

Roosevelt's four elections transformed the American presidency. It revealed how easily a long-standing tradition could give way once a popular incumbent and a national crisis aligned.

Roosevelt's decision to run for a third term stirred controversy. Campaign buttons and literature opposing this break with tradition were widespread both in 1940 and 1944. In 1940, a congressional subcommittee held hearings on "the proprietary of a third term."[61] Wendell Wilkie, the Republican nominee in the 1940 election, promised to pursue a constitutional amendment limiting presidential tenure.[62] This was not the first attempt to do so: between 1789 and 1947, a total of 270 proposals were introduced in Congress seeking to limit

---

59 Quoted in Peabody & Gant, *supra* n. 29 at 585.

60 *Id.* at 588.

61 *Id.* at 586.

62 *Id.*

presidential terms.[63] But despite significant opposition, FDR was elected both in 1940 and 1944.

After Republicans gained control of Congress in 1946, momentum toward mandatory term limits intensified. Even many Democrats supported codifying the Washington–Jefferson precedent following Roosevelt's lengthy service. As historian James Davis noted, the 22nd Amendment arose from the desire of Republicans and Southern Democrats "not to see a repeat performance of four successive presidential victories by another FDR-type candidate."[64]

With this newfound momentum, Congress started deliberations on the 22nd Amendment.

---

63 *Id.* at 590 (Peabody and Gant note that "between 1789 and 1947, 270 proposals to limit the terms of office of the President were introduced in Congress.")

64 James W. Davis, *The American Presidency*, 406 (1995), quoted in Peabody & Gant, *supra* n.29 p. 599.

PART II

THE LEGISLATIVE HISTORY OF THE 22ND AMENDMENT[65]

★ ★ ★

On January 3, 1947, at the opening of the first session of the 80th Congress, House Joint Resolution 27 (H.J. Res. 27) was introduced to propose a constitutional cap of *two elected terms* to the presidency.[66] The House approved the resolution in February 1947 by a substantial margin. When the Senate took it up, Senator Robert Taft added language clarifying succession scenarios: specifically, that a vice president who had served more

65 The detailed account of congressional debates, draft language, and compromise formulations surrounding House Joint Resolution 27 draws substantially on the law review article by Bruce G. Peabody and Scott E. Gant, "The Twice and Future President: Constitutional Interstices and the Twenty-Second Amendment." 83 *Minn. L. Rev.* 565, 568–69 (1999). I did not independently consult original congressional records or archival legislative materials. Rather, I relied on the Peabody & Gant article as a secondary scholarly source summarizing and analyzing that history. I am not aware of any serious academic challenge to their research.

66 U.S. *House Journal*, 80th Congress, Proceedings on H.J. Res. 27 (Jan.–Feb. 1947).

than two years of another president's term would be treated as though he had served a full term for purposes of the limit.[67]

With broad support and without significant public debate, both chambers passed the joint resolution, which was sent to the states on March 21, 1947. Ratification took almost four years. On February 27, 1951, Minnesota became the thirty-sixth state to ratify the proposal, formally enshrining the 22nd Amendment in the Constitution.[68]

Since its adoption in 1951, every president has followed the two-election limit. Eisenhower, Reagan, Clinton, George W. Bush, and Obama all served two terms and stepped down accordingly. Suggestions to repeal the amendment occasionally emerge,[69] but none has gained traction. Although Presidents Eisenhower and Reagan at times voiced support for repealing the amendment,[70] the two-term limit remained largely unquestioned for decades—until recently, when President Trump suggested the possibility of a third term. At the time of writing, President Trump stated that he would not seek one, pointing to the constitutional restriction: "If you read it, it's pretty clear. I'm not allowed to run. It's too bad."[71] He also suggested that finding ways to run would be "too cute."[72]

Whether the amendment is truly "pretty clear" in prohibiting a two-term president from running again has become

---

67 U.S. *Senate Journal*, 80th Congress, floor amendments attributed to Sen. Robert Taft.

68 National Archives record of ratification, Feb. 27, 1951.

69 There have been over fifty proposals to repeal the 22nd Amendment. See Coenen, *infra* n. 89 at 1292.

70 Peabody & Gant, *supra* n.29 at 602-606 (Eisenhower) and at 608 (Reagan)

71 Chris Megerian & Lisa Mascaro, "Trump Says 'It's Too Bad' He Can't Run For A Third Term," AP News, Oct. 29, 2025; https://apnews.com/article/trump-third-term-house-speaker-mike-johnson-2a1702ca962b3d914bd8a216de64bb14.

72 *Id.*

the subject of considerable debate. Surprisingly, the 22nd Amendment is among the least examined by constitutional scholars. The Supreme Court has never ruled directly on it, and most experts have long considered it self-evident that a twice-elected president cannot run for or serve a third term.[73] But what is deemed obvious may not necessarily be correct.

If this issue reaches the courts, the specific language of the 22nd Amendment will be central; after all, constitutional analysis always starts with the text. As previously quoted, the relevant portion of the 22nd Amendment reads:

> No person shall be elected to the office of the President more than twice, and no person who has held the office of President, or acted as President, for more than two years of a term to which some other person was elected President shall be elected to the office of the President more than once.[74]

As discussed in the Introduction, this wording leaves open a substantial loophole. On its face, a president who has already been elected twice may still *serve* a third term—as long as he is not *elected* to it. Thus, if a former two-term president were to ascend to the office by means *other than election*, the text does not clearly forbid it.

This raises a central historical question: What did the drafters intend? Why did they employ the phrase "elected to the office," rather than stating that a two-term president would be

---

73 For a literature review, see Peabody & Gant, *supra* n.29 at 567 n. 7.

74 The amendment includes a grandfather clause for President Truman and for vice presidents: "But this Article shall not apply to any person holding the office of President when this Article was proposed by the Congress, and shall not prevent any person who may be holding the office of President, or acting as President, during the term within which this Article becomes operative from holding the office of President or acting as President during the remainder of such term."

"ineligible," as found in the 12th Amendment; or using more comprehensive wording such as "hold office," as used in Article II; or "acting as president," as used in the 22nd Amendment itself; or "serve," which would have provided the broadest possible prohibition? The choice of the narrower prohibition has generated enduring, if not always well considered, questions and is explored further below. It also leads to the question, sometimes raised in other contexts—whether text or intent (or purpose) should govern if and when there is a conflict between the two.

Chapter 3

A Closer Look at the Legislative History

★ ★ ★

The most surprising fact about the legislative history of the 22nd Amendment is that Congress initially considered quite different and more comprehensive prohibitions, which it subsequently abandoned for the text that we have now—a text that exclusively focuses on presidential elections.

When House Judiciary Chairman Earl Michener and Speaker of the House Joseph Martin introduced *House Joint Resolution 27* (H.J. Res. 27) on January 3, 1947,[75] it stated originally:

> [no] person *shall be chosen or serve* as President of the United States for any term, *or be eligible to hold* the office of President during any term, if such person shall have heretofore served as President during the whole or any part of each of any two separate terms.[76]

---

75 U.S. *House Journal*, 80th Congress, Proceedings on H.J. Res. 27 (Jan.–Feb. 1947).

76 See 93 *Congressional Record* 47-48 (1947) (own emphasis). Quoted in Peabody & Gant, *supra* n.29 at 593.

The House Judiciary Committee later revised the language and presented an updated version on February 5:

> Any person who has served as President of the United States during all, or portions, of any two terms, *shall therefore be ineligible to hold* the office of President.

This revision did not materially change the earlier draft: under both versions, whether a president was elected or assumed office through other means, he could not serve more than two terms.

The Senate received the revised resolution on February 6 and referred it to the Judiciary Committee, which adjusted the language again:

> A person who has held the office of the President, or acted as President, on three hundred and sixty-five calendar days or more in each of two terms *shall not be eligible to hold* the office of the President, or to act as President, for any part of another term.[77]

Like the earlier House proposals, this formulation addressed presidential *service* broadly, not merely the number of electoral victories. Had this version been adopted, no reasonable debate could exist today about whether a twice-elected president could serve again—such service would have been clearly barred by the unambiguous text of the amendment.

On March 10, the Senate considered an amendment by Democratic Senator Warren Magnuson, designed to replace the Committee's more complex language. Magnuson proposed

---

77 S. Rep. No. 80-34 at 1 (1947) (own emphasis). Quoted in Peabody & Gant, *supra* n.29 at 594.

the simpler phrase: "no person shall be elected to the office of President more than twice."[78] He justified this by stating that the "only purpose [of his amendment] is to make it simple so that the people of the United States will know what they are voting on when it is presented to the States."[79] While acknowledging that his wording did not expressly address non-electoral accession to the presidency, Magnuson minimized the concern, emphasizing that Congress's primary goal was to restrict the number of times a person could be elected. Magnuson explained that his version "could be easily understood by everyone and would not involve complicated legal questions . . . such as "When is a man Acting President? When does he assume office" and "to what period he should be limited" when "elevated to the office of President through circumstances beyond his control?"[80] In other words, Magnuson was aware of potential loopholes that his proposed language may create but made the practical judgment that such scenarios are so unlikely that it may be worth the risk. His reasoning leaves much to be desired. If he wanted clarity, simplicity, and unambiguity, the word "serve" satisfies those criteria far better than the word "elected."

Senator Joseph Tydings, one of the proponents of the version ultimately adopted, supported Magnuson's approach. He argued: "What we are trying to do is to stop any man from being elected President more than twice. . . . But under the committee amendment a man could be prohibited from being elected President more than once, provided that he had served

---

78 93 *Congressional Record* 1863 (1947). Quoted in Peabody & Gant, *supra* n.29 at 595.

79 *Id.* at 1865. Quoted in Peabody & Gant, p. 595 n. 145.

80 *Id.* at 1863. Quoted in Peabody & Gant, p. 595.

more than 1 year prior to the time he was elected President. . . . I think that provision is a little stringent."[81]

Opposition soon arose. Senator Bourke Hickenlooper argued that Magnuson's wording would create a "peculiar situation" whereby "an individual who becomes President, by accident, and act of divine providence, or otherwise, and who was not originally elected to the position, is the only person who can hold protracted office in the Presidency"[82] In other words, a person who assumed office without election could theoretically serve for extended periods. Senator Robert Taft raised a similar concern, noting that such a person might be eligible for two full elections thereafter and thus "serve as long as 11½ years—too long."[83]

In response to the concerns that were expressed, Senator Taft introduced a compromise amendment on March 12, which combined the clarity of Magnuson's approach with language addressing succession:

> No person shall be elected to the office of the President more than twice, and no person who has held the office of president or acted as President for more than 2 years of a term to which some other person was elected President, shall be *elected* to the office of the President more than once.[84]

This compromise language was ultimately adopted and now appears in the 22nd Amendment. Notably, the final text diverges substantially from earlier drafts that would have rendered a

81 *Id.* Quoted in Peabody & Gant, *supra* n.29 at 596.

82 93 *Congressional Record* 1864 (1947). Quoted in Peabody & Gant, p. 596.

83 Quoted in Peabody & Gant, *supra* n.29 p. 597.

84 *Id.*

two-term president fully *ineligible to hold the office* under any circumstances.

Thus, the question arises: if Congress was aware of more comprehensive alternatives, why did it opt for the narrower language centered solely on *election*? Was this an intentional allowance for the possibility—however remote—of a non-electoral third term?

Bruce Peabody and Scott Gant, in their well-researched article "*The Twice and Future President: Constitutional Interstices and the Twenty-Second Amendment*," suggest that the shift reflected political compromise rather than deliberate policy design:

> [O]ur review of the congressional debates suggests that the text of the Amendment was probably shaped by the impulse of compromise. The shift from the House's reference to presidential "service" and "tenure" to the Senate's eventual reliance on simply limiting presidential "election" appears largely to have been a function of political give-and-take.[85]

They note that Senator Taft himself acknowledged his amendment was intended to strike a balance between supporters and critics of Magnuson's proposal. Similarly, when the House later considered the version endorsed by the Senate, some expressed concern that it was "pregnant with questions" and would have preferred the original wording, but ultimately accepted the need for "compromise" as part of legislative process.[86]

Peabody and Gant conclude:

> Th[e] willingness to compromise may have contributed to

85 *Id.* at, p. 600.

86 Peabody & Gant, p. 600 (quoting Sen. Michener).

> the imprecision that characterized the language used by members of Congress as they considered [Resolution 27] and its various formulations. Members of both the House and the Senate . . . often vaguely suggested that they were attempting to limit presidential "tenure" without elaborating exactly what they had in mind or using the term consistently . . .
>
> And . . . those debating the Amendment at times appeared to conflate the notion of "election" with the other ways in which a President might come to serve, but at other moments they clearly distinguished elections from non-electoral means of assuming the Office of the President.
>
> Furthermore, congressional interest in not "penalizing" those unelected but nonetheless called upon to serve or act as President led Congress to focus on "elections" as the cornerstone of the Amendment's proscriptions—a focus that prohibited only *reelection* of an already twice-elected President. In prohibiting "reelection" only, Congress seemingly glossed over the significance of limiting subsequent election rather than subsequent "service," and unwittingly. . . . left open the possibility of a previously twice-elected President reassuming Office to again serve (or act) as President."[87]

Turning to the ultimate question of legislative intent, while Congress clearly meant to restrict presidential tenure due to fears of "an executive dynasty,"[88] there is no compelling evidence that legislators intended to authorize a route for a twice-elected president to reclaim office via non-electoral means. However, the record indicates that Congress was fully aware

87 Peabody & Gant, p. 600.

88 S. Rep. No. 80-34 at 2 (1947). Quoted in Bruce G. Peabody, "The Twice and Future President Revisited: Of Three Term Presidents and Constitutional End Runs," 101 *Minnesota Law Review Headnotes*, 121, 137 (2016).

of the constitutional distinctions between elections and other succession mechanisms.

Importantly, the sitting president at the time, Harry Truman, had himself become president through succession after FDR's death. In addition, prior generations had repeatedly witnessed unelected presidents assuming office. Moreover, although Congress initially considered drafts employing broader legal terminology, it ultimately adopted language limited to electoral pathways. As a result, deciphering legislative intent beyond the broad desire to prevent extended incumbency remains speculative. It is in the nature of political compromises that they often elevate immediate results over longer term considerations. What Congress plainly intended was to get the amendment enacted quickly. In doing so, the agreed-on language that left open the possibility of a non-elected third term—through several of the mechanisms suggested earlier.

Professor Dan Coenen, in his analysis of the legislative history of the 22nd Amendment,[89] confirms that virtually no attention was given to the effect of the proposed amendment on the vice presidency. The debate focused solely on presidential elections, not vice-presidential elections.

One proposed draft—submitted by Senator Wilbert Lee O' Daniel—would have expressly extended the limitation to both offices, providing that "no person who shall have served as President *or Vice President* shall be eligible for election to the office of President *or the office of Vice President*." Congress rejected this language by a 1–82 vote, a decisive repudiation.[90]

Does this mean Congress intended *not* to restrict election of a twice-elected president to the vice presidency? Not

89 Dan Coenen, "Two-Time Presidents and the Vice Presidency" 56 *Boston College Law Review* 1287 (2015).

90 *Id.* at 1301 n.73.

necessarily. As Professor Coenen explains, the legislative history reflects an effort to balance two competing concerns rather than to speak directly to that issue. On one side were those who worried that rigid term limits might deprive Americans of the opportunity to choose the leader they felt best suited to guide the nation—especially in moments of crisis, echoing the arguments Alexander Hamilton had raised in the Constitutional Convention and *The Federalist Papers*.[91] In contrast, others feared a drift toward a presidency resembling a hereditary or indefinite tenure—concerns fueled by Franklin D. Roosevelt's four-term precedent.[92]

The Magnuson–Taft amendments ultimately provided the compromise that broke the congressional impasse and pushed the 22nd Amendment across the finish line. As Professor Coenen explains:

> Neither Senator Taft nor any other House or Senate member, however, expressed any concern about electing a former President as Vice-President, and the reason why is apparent: This possibility was far removed from the sort

---

91 *Id.* at 1303 n.79 (quoting Sen. Pepper: "what is proposed here is to limit the right and the power of the American people in a moment of great crisis . . . to elect a man . . . whom they deem best fitted to lead them through the crucial time."; Sen. Kilgore: limiting terms "might deprive the American people of the services of the best man in any emergency." *Id.*at 1948; Sen. Holland: "I should hate to have the Nation put in the position that such a person could not be called back to the Presidency." ; Sen. Lucas: "I consider the proposal dangerous to our liberties." *Id.* at 1778 and Sen. Hill: "[T]he pending amendment to the Constitution would place the wisdom of the people in a straight-jacket." *Id.* at 1771).

92 *Id.* at 1308 n. 114 (quoting Sen. Lucas: "the breaking of the two-term precedent by Franklin D. Roosevelt . . . is the basic reason for seeking this constitutional amendment."; Rep. Smith: "we do not want to impose upon our country again one-man government such as we have had for the past 14 years."; Rep. Jenkins: "The tenure of Franklin D. Roosevelt proved that Washington and Jefferson were wise.")

> of overreaching that reformers perceived in the actions of Franklin Roosevelt. Put simply, when the Magnuson revision cropped up, Senator Taft and his Republican colleagues kept their eyes on the prize. They recognized that the phrasing of either the Senate Judiciary Committee draft or the Magnuson proposal would block self-perpetuating reelections by a single person to the presidency itself. That was the crux of the reformers' agenda. That was what they sought. That is what they got. But they got nothing more. They got nothing more because the language they accepted from the Magnuson revision took them only that far.[93]

In short, the compromise was designed to prevent indefinite reelection to the presidency—nothing more. It resolved the legislative stalemate by targeting the specific concern that had driven the amendment: Franklin Roosevelt's unprecedented election to four consecutive terms. The compromise language imposed a restriction only on *election* to the presidency, leaving untouched other possible avenues of service, including the vice presidency.

The record does not demonstrate a deliberate intent either to permit or to prohibit a twice-elected president from subsequently serving as vice president. Rather, the drafters focused narrowly on preventing repeated electoral accession to the presidency. Anything beyond that is a matter of conjecture—not specific or historically mandated legislative intent.

To the extent the final draft became the 22nd Amendment reflected a desire for clarity that could easily be understood by the public, it failed. The final product is anything but unambiguous.

Its confusing and somewhat contradictory history supports

---

93 *Id.* at 1307-1308.

the argument for focusing on the actual text arrived at after the conflicting proposals were considered, debated, and rejected. Ultimately, the ratified language is the only objective certainty.

Chapter 4

The Academic Debate

★ ★ ★

The current discussion was reanimated by the suggestion—from President Trump and some of his supporters—of the possibility of a third term. This has prompted renewed examination of the 22nd Amendment.[94] The most prominent argument supporting the possibility of a non-electoral third term originates from Bruce Peabody and Scott Gant, who contend that a twice-elected president could still *ascend* to the presidency if not *elected* to it.[95]

Most legal scholars disagree. Michael Dorf of Cornell Law School told the *Washington Post*, "What the 22nd Amendment does is prohibit him from being elected for a third term, rather than serving for a third term—which I regard as an unfortunate

94 See, e.g., Leo Sands, "Can Trump Run for a Third Term? The 22nd Amendment Flatly Prevents It," *Washington Post*, March 31, 2025; Jacob Gershman, "Could Trump Serve A Third Term as President: The Constitution Forbids His Election Against, but Another Path Isn't Entirely Foreclosed, Some Scholars Say," *Wall Street Journal*, March 31, 2025.

95 For this view, see also Dan Coenen, "Two-Time Presidents and the Vice Presidency" 56 *Boston College Law Review* 1287 (2015), *supra* n. 89.

drafting error."[96] Dorf provided little intellectual support for his assertion. The claim that the provision reflects a "drafting error" ultimately turns on what Congress intended, which as explained above, is considerably more ambiguous than his account acknowledges.

Others, including Yale Law School's Akhil Amar and Bruce Ackerman, shift focus from the drafters' intent to the people's understanding of the amendment. Professor Ackerman argues that a twice-elected president cannot serve again because the amendment "represents a considered judgment by the American people, after Franklin Roosevelt's lengthy stay in the White House" to limit presidential tenure to "two elected terms"[97] Professor Amar similarly states that the amendment constitutes a "self-imposed" limitation "resulting from a broadly inclusive democratic process featuring a series of extraordinary votes" to prevent entrenchment and encourage "a healthy rotation."[98]

Although these arguments are better considered than Dorf's, they still leave much to speculation and surmise; determining what the public actually understood at the time remains complicated and speculative. As one contemporary account described the state ratification process, the amendment "glided through legislatures in a fog of silence . . . without hearings, without publicity, without any of that popular participation that should have accompanied a change in the organic law of the country."[99] Perhaps that was because it was

---

96 Leo Sands, "Can Trump Run for a Third Term? The 22nd Amendment Flatly Prevents It," *Washington Post*, March 31, 2025.

97 Bruce A. Ackerman, *Before the Next Attack*, p. 204 n. 34 (2006).

98 Akhil R. Amar, "The Supreme Court 1999 Term—Foreword: The Document and the Doctrine," 114 *Harv. L. Rev.* 26, 37 (2000).

99 "The Two-Term Limit," *Nation*, March 10, 1951, at 216-217 (quoted in Peabody, "The Twice and Future President Revisited," 2016 at p. 140).

clear that the public wanted this change, but absent widespread debate, that too is surmise—perhaps well-grounded but less than the degree of certainty that should be required to ignore the text.

What would public opinion have been if the citizens were presented with a test case, such as the following: Both the president and vice president are killed in a terrorist attack precipitating an international crisis: the two next-in-line legislators are unequipped to govern,[100] but the secretary of state, being a two-term former president, is perfectly suited to take over. Is it clear that public opinion would overwhelmingly reject a literal interpretation of the 22nd Amendment that would prohibit this qualified leader from serving or acting as an unelected president?

Even if such a common understanding by the American public could be firmly established, there is still the question of whether it *should* override the constitutional text. We will consider that question in a subsequent chapter.

The 12th Amendment

A question related to the succession issue discussed above is whether the 12th Amendment would prevent a twice-elected president from becoming vice president and then becoming president. The 12th Amendment, enacted back in 1804, states that "no person constitutionally *ineligible* to the office of President shall be eligible to that of Vice-President." (own emphasis).

Adopted to prevent electoral deadlocks like those in 1796 and 1800, the 12th Amendment modified the Electoral

100 The Speaker of the House and the president pro tempore of the Senate are next in line. Presidential succession is discussed *infra* pp. 99–100.

College so that the president and vice president are chosen separately.[101]

Prior to the enactment of the 12th Amendment, electors would cast two votes for President, and the runner up would become vice president (sometimes the president's political nemesis).

In the contentious election of 1800, Thomas Jefferson and Aaron Burr received the same number of electoral votes, triggering a deadlock that required thirty-six ballots in the House of Representatives to determine the winner. Alexander Hamilton—despite deep ideological disagreement with Jefferson—intervened to secure his election, concluding that Jefferson was more principled and trustworthy than Burr, who became vice president once Jefferson was elected. Hamilton's distrust of Burr proved prescient: while serving as vice president, Burr fatally shot Hamilton in a duel. Burr was indicted for murder in both New York and New Jersey but was never prosecuted and was subsequently removed from Jefferson's ticket in 1804. At Jefferson's urging, he was later charged with treason. In that trial, the jury concluded that he was "not proved to be guilty," reflecting Chief Justice Marshall's stringent evidentiary interpretation of treason. When Burr sought to have the conclusion changed to simply "not guilty," Marshall refused,

---

101 Almost a century later, the disputed presidential election of 1876 between Rutherford B. Hayes and Samuel J. Tilden triggered another constitutional crisis, as competing slates of electors from multiple states led to an unresolved electoral deadlock that persisted until just days before Inauguration Day. To break the impasse, Congress created a bipartisan Electoral Commission, whose decision ultimately awarded the presidency to Hayes pursuant to a political compromise rather than clear constitutional guidance. The controversy led to the passage of the Electoral Count Act of 1887, which sought to codify procedures to prevent such disputes from recurring. While the Act mitigated some of the risks of electoral deadlock, recurring controversies over vote counting and certification in more recent elections suggest that the underlying structural vulnerabilities have not been fully resolved.

holding that the jury's narrow formulation properly reflected the constitutional standard and the insufficiency of the government's evidence.[102]

Although the Burr–Hamilton duel did not itself prompt the 12th Amendment, the intense personal and political conflict between the two men stemmed from the deadlock in the 1800 election—the very crisis that the 12th Amendment was designed to prevent.

The 12th Amendment refers to the minimum qualification requirements of Article II, Section, clause 5, according to which presidents must be natural born citizens, thirty-five years of age, and with fourteen years of US residency. Through its interaction with the 22nd Amendment, the 12th Amendment has been interpreted by some to make any person who is ineligible to be vice president also ineligible to succeed to the presidency.[103] As Professor Matthew Frank explains,

> [s]ince the ordinary path to the presidency contemplated by the Constitution is via the ballots of . . . electors, then by any ordinary mode of legal reasoning, the 22nd Amendment changed the answer to the question—who is "constitutionally ineligible to the office of President"? . . . Now the class includes aliens, immigrants, citizens under thirty-five, others failing the presidency requirement, *and persons previously elected twice (or having served one term elected and more than*

102 "Chief Justice John Marshall's Judicial Statesmanship Amid in Re Burr: A Pragmatic Political Balancing Against President Jefferson Over Treason," 53 *UIC J. Marshall L. Rev.* 789, 899 (2021). ("Marshall likely suspected that an acquittal that bore a sufficient muddiness would maintain American posterity for the Court and the greater nation. . . . Marshall's careful outcomes was one in which the Court established that Burr was legally innocent, but perhaps morally guilty.")

103 See e.g., Richard Albert, "The Constitutional Politics of Presidential Succession," 39 *Hofstra L. Rev.* 497, 565-566 (2011).

half of another's term after succeeding from the vice presidency—another requirement of the 22nd Amendment).[104]

However, this argument risks circularity. Since the 22nd Amendment restricts *election*, not succession, it is unclear why a twice-elected president is necessarily ineligible to become vice president through non-electoral pathways.

The 22nd Amendment only deals with "electability," while the 12th Amendment deals with "eligibility." According to some prominent scholars, "eligible" and "electable" mean the same thing. For example, Professor Amar contends that *eligible* and *electable* share the same Latin root and that dictionaries in circulation when the 12th Amendment was adopted included *electable* among the definitions for *eligible*.[105] As Professor Coenen wryly observes, the shared Latin root is not helpful. "The words 'centipedes' and 'centenarian' have a shared Latin root," i.e., "cent" meaning one hundred, "[b]ut that shared fact hardly means that a bug and an old person are the same thing."[106]

Even accepting Professor's Amar's linguistic premise, the logic does not resolve the problem. A twice-elected president might still serve as president (and is thus eligible to be vice president) if he were to assume the office through non-election—for instance, by becoming Speaker of the House and succeeding to office following simultaneous vacancy due to death, resignation, or impeachment. The statute that determines the order of succession to the presidency provides that the person selected must not be "under disability to discharge the powers and duties

104 Matthew J. Frank, "Constitutional Sleight of Hand," *National Review*, July 31, 2007, available at https://www.nationalreview.com/bench-memos/constitutional-sleight-hand-matthew-j-franck/.

105 Akhil Amar, *America's Constitution: A Biography* 662 n. 8 (2006), p. 128-129.

106 Dan Coenen, "Two-Time Presidents and the Vice Presidency" p. 1296 n. 42.

of the office of the President" or must not "fail to qualify" for that office.[107] This of course begs the question whether a two-term president who is serving as Speaker is under "a disability" to discharge the powers and duties of the presidency or "fails to qualify" for that office if he is not "elected" to it. Neither the statute nor the Constitution answers that question beyond reiterating the only textual disqualification—namely being *elected* for a third term.

The eminent professor and judge, Richard Posner, offers an answer that applies only to a two-term president who then seeks the vice presidency as part of a plan to have him become president upon the resignation of the elected president. Posner argued that "read literally," the 22nd Amendment allows former presidents serve as vice presidents. But under the 22nd Amendment, "elected to the office of the president more than twice" should apply to any person elected to the vice presidency who subsequently takes office as president, since such a person was elected with the presumption of being able to serve in the office of the presidency. As Posner puts it, "electing a vice president means electing a vice president and contingently electing him as president. That interpretation, though a little bold, would honor the intention behind the 22nd Amendment."[108]

It is a clever argument that produces the result Posner wants, but it is far too speculative and inferential to provide a definite resolution to the issues surrounding the intent and purpose of the 22nd Amendment. Moreover, it would not preclude a two-term president from being *selected* rather than *elected* as

---

107 Presidential Succession Act of 1947.

108 Peter Baker, "VP Bill? Depends on Meaning of 'Elected,'" *Washington Post*, Oct. 19, 2006.

vice president—as occurred when Gerald Ford and Nelson Rockefeller each assumed the vice presidency without election.

In commentary appearing after Trump's remarks reignited debate, Princeton's Deborah Pearlstein told *The Washington Post* that the 12th Amendment "closes the door" to any route by which Trump could regain office via the vice presidency. According to her, "Trump is constitutionally ineligible to serve a third term. End of story."[109]

My former colleague Laurence Tribe—whom I have often criticized for allowing partisan biases to color his interpretation of constitutional issues involving President Trump—displayed commendable intellectual consistency when he wrote that neither the 22nd nor the 12th Amendment definitively resolves the issue. In a post on X dated March 31, 2025, Professor Tribe stated:

> Anyone discounting a 3d Trump term per the 22d am + the 12th am is thinking magically: The 22d dsn't bar *serving* a 3d term, only being *elected* 3 times. The 12th dsn't bar running for VP unless "ineligible" to serve as Pres, but Trump isn't ineligible. QED![110]

Professor Tribe is not only thinking what his colleague Professor Feldman regards as "unthinkable,"[111] he appears to be agreeing with my thought experiment on the issue.

My constitutional analysis that follows reflects an effort—however imperfect—to apply a consistent interpretive framework without regard to partisan considerations.

---

109 Leo Sands, "Can Trump Run for a Third Term? The 22nd Amendment Flatly Prevents It," *Washington Post*, March 31, 2025.

110 Tribe tweeted on March 31, 2025.

111 See my discussion of Professor's Feldman position, *supra* at pp. 5–7.

PART III

MY OWN CONSTITUTIONAL ANALYSIS

★ ★ ★

Chapter 5

Any Constitutional Interpretation Must Start (Yet Not Necessarily End) with the Text

★ ★ ★

When interpreting a constitutional provision, no serious judge or scholar would dispute that analysis must begin with the text.

Textualism—a school of thought linked to the late Justice Scalia and others—maintains that constitutional analysis must begin, and, where the language is unambiguous, end there as well, reflecting the language adopted by the people through Article V (the amendment process under the US Constitution). Its central premise is that the role of the courts is to apply what the Constitution *says*, not what its drafters *might have meant* or what modern actors wish it had said. Justice Scalia wrote that consulting external sources to discern congressional intent is generally unnecessary because "it is the law that governs, not the intent of the lawgiver."[112] He was skeptical of legislative

112 Antonin Scalia, *A Matter of Interpretation: Federal Courts and the Law*, 17 (1997).

history, believing it enables judges, "under the guise or even the self-delusion of pursuing unexpressed legislative intent," to "pursue their own objectives and desires."[113] Justice Scalia famously said in speeches that looking at legislative history is like "walking into a crowded cocktail party and looking over the heads of the guests to pick out your friends."[114]

Yet many constitutional provisions are ambiguous, unclear, cryptic, open-ended, and subject to multiple reasonable interpretations. Human language—especially legal and political language—cannot fully capture the complexity or nuance of human thought, action, and interaction.[115] Textualism alone cannot always bridge this gap.

Oliver Wendell Holmes Jr. recognized this truth when he wrote: "A word is not a crystal, transparent and unchanged, it is the skin of a living thought and may vary greatly in color and content according to the circumstances and time in which it is used."[116] Lewis Carroll, in a more whimsical way, illustrates the same insight in *Alice's Adventures in Wonderland*. When Humpty Dumpty insists that a word "means just what I choose it to mean—neither more nor less," Alice responds, pointedly, "That's a great deal to make one word mean." Humpty Dumpty replies that when he makes a word do that much work, he "always pay[s] it extra."[117] Some constitutional words indeed demand "overtime pay." "Elected" is not such a word. It has a precise meaning different than "serve," "act," or "hold," as

113 *Id.* at 17–18.

114 Antonin Scalia & Bryan A. Garner, *Reading Law: The Interpretation of Legal Texts* 377 (2012). (The quotation is attributed to Judge Harold Leventhal of the United States Court of Appeals for the D.C. Circuit).

115 See Alan M. Dershowitz, "The Relationship Among Language, Morality, and Law: The Chicken and the Egg," 52 *Florida State University Law Review* 739 (2026).

116 *Towne v. Eisner*, 245 U.S. 418, 425, 38 S. Ct. 158, 159, 62 L. Ed. 372 (1918).

117 Lewis Carroll, *The Annotated Alice* (New York: Norton, 2000), p. 213.

determined by case law that was known to the drafters of the 22nd Amendment.

Indeed, the Supreme Court's own interpretative approach supports this distinction.[118] The Supreme Court has called it the "normal rule of statutory construction"[119] that "identical words used in different parts of the same act are intended to have the same meaning"[120] and, conversely, "where words differ" the Court presumes that "the drafter has acted intentionally and purposefully."[121] Under these principles of statutory construction, the Court would expect the words "elected," "serve," "act," and "hold" to carry different meanings—and would treat them accordingly.

Originalism—a related interpretive approach represented by Professor Amar, Professor Randy Barnett, and others—holds that constitutional language should be understood as it was at the time of adoption. Yet it is not always easy to retrieve those understandings or to apply them to a legal or political system that has changed dramatically over centuries.

For example, the prohibition against "cruel and unusual punishments" in the Eighth Amendment was drafted before long-term incarceration was the primary method of punishment; the punishments of the time included death and branding, not life

---

118 See the excellent discussion in Dan Coenen's article "Two-Time Presidents and the Vice Presidency," *supra* n. 89 at 1296.

119 Rules of statutory construction typically also apply to the Constitution. See e.g., *Badger v. Hoidale*, 88 F.2d 208, 2011 (8th Cir. 1937) ("[R]ules governing the construction of statutes are applicable to the construction of the Constitution.").

120 *Gustafson v. Alloyd Co.*, 513 U.S. 561, 570, Department of Revenue of *Ore. v. ACF Industries, Inc.*, 510 U.S. 332, 342, 114 S.Ct. 843, 849, 127 L.Ed.2d 165 (1994); see also *Brooke Group Ltd. v. Brown & Williamson Tobacco Corp.*, 509 U.S. 209, 230, (1993); *Atlantic Cleaners & Dyers, Inc. v. United States*, 286 U.S. 427, 433 (1932).

121 *Burlington N. & Santa Fe Ry. Co. v. White*, 548 U.S. 53, 61-67 (2006). See also *Russello v. U.S.* 464 U.S. 16, 23-24 (1983).

imprisonment for repeated minor offenses under modern "three strikes" laws.[122] Another example from criminal law—the subject I taught for five decades at Harvard Law School—is the understanding of "trial by jury" at the founding clearly contemplated a unanimous twelve-man jury of property-owning, Christian white males. Yet the Supreme Court until recently permitted non-unanimous, six-person juries consisting of individuals far from the original framers' expectations.[123] These examples illustrate that certain constitutional phrases were drafted with a level of abstraction that presupposed interpretive evolution.

At the same time, the Framers unquestionably knew how to write unambiguous, self-contained provisions that leave very little interpretive discretion to future judges. The Constitution requires that treaties be ratified by "two thirds of the Senators present,"[124] not by a "supermajority" or "substantial consensus." The Seventh Amendment requires a jury trial in cases where the "value in controversy" exceeds "twenty dollars." It does not say that the amount must be "considerable" or "substantial." Perhaps foolishly, the Framers wrote "twenty dollars"—not even adjusted for inflation![125] It would make sense to interpret "twenty dollars"

---

122 In 2012, California passed Proposition 36 which eliminated life sentences for non-serious, non-violent crimes and established procedures for inmates sentenced to life in prison for minor third-strike crimes to petition courts for reduced sentences. Prior to Proposition 36, defendants have been given life sentences for minor, non-violent offenses including stealing one dollar in loose change from a parked car and possessing less than a gram of narcotics. See Stanford Law School, "Three Strikes Basics," available at https://law.stanford.edu/three-strikes-project/three-strikes-basics/.

123 See *Ramos v. Louisiana*, 590 U.S. 83 (2020) overturning *Apodoca v. Oregon*, 406 U.S. 404 (1972) and *Johnson v. Louisiana*, 406 U.S. 356 (1972). Prior to the decision, Oregon and Louisiana allowed non-unanimous jury convictions, while all other states had incorporated the unanimous requirement.

124 See Article II of the U.S. Constitution.

125 Madison's original draft left the amount blank. The twenty-dollar amount was subsequently added. See U.S. Constitution amend. VII, Jury Trial in Civil Cases, in Constitution Annotated (Library of Congress), available at https://www.govinfo.gov/content/pkg/GPO-CONAN-1992/pdf/GPO-CONAN-1992-10-8.pdf. p. 1452 n. 6.

to mean the *current* value of that amount, but no theory of constitutional interpretation would allow that.

Or take the age requirements in the Constitutional text. The age requirements for federal office—thirty-five for the president,[126] thirty for senators,[127] twenty-five for representatives[128]—are not phrased in terms of "maturity" or "experience." If a thirty-year-old produces legislative history showing that the intent is to ensure maturity to run for president and he produces unchallenged evidence that he is mature beyond his chronological age, such history, even if clear, cannot be considered because the text is unambiguous. I do not know of any legal scholar or judge who would disagree with this. These provisions seem to be self-defining and not subject to judicial modification based on legislative intent, changing circumstances or policy considerations.[129]

Most debates about constitutional interpretation involve open-ended provisions such as "due process of law," "equal protection of the laws," "cruel and unusual punishments," "excessive bail," and "unreasonable searches and seizures."

---

126 Art. II, Sec 1 of the U.S. Constitution.

127 Art. I, Sec 3 of the U.S. Constitution.

128 Art. I, Sec 2 of the U.S. Constitution.

129 In the Chinese culture, newborn babies are already considered to be one year old (which would make me eighty-eight years!) From an originalist standpoint, it is worth noting that while average life expectancy in the late eighteenth century was skewed downward due to high childhood mortality, healthy adults (including the Framers) routinely lived into their sixties. Today, with average life expectancy approaching eighty, longevity and sustained cognitive capacity make extended political careers significantly more plausible. Thus, the practical context in which presidential term limits now operate is markedly different from that understood by the generation that ratified the 12th and even the 22nd Amendment. In contemporary terms, a leader such as JD Vance—who would be only in his early fifties at the close of two terms as president—could remain credible for national leadership roles decades later. Yet despite this demographic shift, I do not know any purposivist who would read the age requirements in the Constitution not literally.

Scholars and judges argue over whether interpretation should depend on the framers' specific intent, their general purpose, broader constitutional structure, or evolving societal needs. I have engaged in this debate both as a scholar and as a litigator.[130]

But the question posed by the 22nd Amendment is fundamentally different from these standard interpretive disputes, as will now be discussed.

130 See, e.g., Alan M. Dershowitz, *Is There A Right to Remain Silent*, Chapter 3: "The Limits of Textual Analysis in Constitutional Interpretation" (2008).

Chapter 6

The 22nd Amendment Raises an Unusual Question

★ ★ ★

As previously emphasized, the text of that amendment restricts only the *reelection* of an already twice-elected president. On its face, the text does not (1) limit the number of times, consecutively or cumulatively, a president may *serve*, *act*, or *hold office*—words that the drafters of the 22nd Amendment clearly knew as they are literally in the amendment and related texts—or (2) prohibit such a person from reassuming the presidency by means *other than* election. Yet the legislative history shows that the drafters of the 22nd Amendment presumably intended to prohibit a two-term president from serving a third term under any circumstances.

If these two underlying conclusions are correct—first, that the unambiguous text prohibits only being *elected* more than twice, and therefore does not bar a twice-elected president from *serving* again via succession; and second, that the framers of the amendment intended to prohibit such a president from *serving* again under any circumstances—then we confront a stark and rare interpretive dilemma: what should a court do when the clear text of a constitutional provision directly contradicts what appears to be the clear intent and purpose of the drafters?

While the 22nd Amendment text is not as unquestionably unambiguous as the age requirements in the Constitution or the "value in controversy" clause found in the Seventh Amendment, it is far clearer than many constitutional provisions. It prohibits, unambiguously, a two-term president being "elected," not "serving," "holding office," or "acting." Under such circumstances, can a court reasonably interpret "elected" to mean "serve," "hold," or "act," especially when the Constitution uses those different words intentionally elsewhere—and when previous drafts of this very amendment used such broader prohibitory terms, and were explicitly rejected? Can judges reinterpret or essentially rewrite the word "elected" to mean the quite dissimilar and rejected words "serve," "hold" or "act"? Put more sharply: Can the intent or purpose of a constitutional amendment ever override—or (pardon the pun) "trump"—its text? These are questions that are rarely discussed by academics or decided by judges, because so direct a conflict has rarely arisen. But the 22nd Amendment raises such a conflict, and it must be considered.

CHAPTER 7

When Text and Purpose Are in Conflict: Which Should Prevail?

★ ★ ★

Purposivists, such as my friend and colleague Justice Stephen Breyer,[131] argue that when the *text* is subject to multiple interpretations, its *purpose*—if it can reasonably be discerned—should determine which of these plausible interpretations prevails. When the *text* is *unambiguous* and subject to only one reasonable interpretation, the *text* should prevail—unless the textual interpretation is utterly absurd (however that is defined).

For instance, even though "natural born citizen" may literally mean born *in* the United States, it would be absurd to deny that status to a person born to American parents who were serving abroad in the American army when he or she was born. So the phrase "natural born citizen" has been broadened—essentially rewritten—to include several categories of citizens who were literally born outside the borders of the

131 See e.g., Stephen Breyer, *Active Liberty: Interpreting Our Democratic Constitution* (2005).

country and thus not naturally born within these borders, but under circumstances to make them indistinguishable in every meaningful way from those born to similarly situated parents who happen to be in the country at the time of the birth.[132]

This tension between textualism and purposivism often arises in statutory interpretation. The Supreme Court has acknowledged that even seemingly clear constitutional language may require adjustment—though critics would say rewriting—to avoid outcomes inconsistent with broader statutory or constitutional structure. Accordingly, before turning to policy objections to a third-term president, it is necessary to consider whether a textual approach alone adequately addresses the 22nd Amendment.

The Court has sometimes interpreted legal language beyond its literal meaning to honor perceived legislative intent. Most notably, in the 1892 case of *Church of the Holy Trinity v. United States*,[133] it declined to apply the statute's literal terms because doing so would have contradicted what it regarded as Congress's intended purpose: to restrict the importation of manual laborers, not clergy, notwithstanding the statute's broad language. In that opinion (now best known for declaring the US a "Christian nation"[134]), Justice David Brewer articulated a long-standing interpretive principle: "A thing may be within the letter of the statute and yet not within the statute, because not within its spirit, nor within the intention of its makers."[135]

---

132 At the time of this writing, the Trump administration, through an executive order, is trying to narrow the meaning of birthright citizenship by claiming that it is not intended to apply to children of undocumented parents. See Amy Howe, "Trump asks Supreme Court to Step in on Birthright Citizenship," SCOTUSblog.com, March 14, 2025.

133 *Holy Trinity Church v. United States*, 143 U.S. 457 (1892).

134 *Id.* at 471.

135 *Id.* at 459.

For decades, *Holy Trinity* was widely cited as the paradigmatic example of purposivism even as later courts and commentators came to criticize it as an instance of "legislating from the bench." Justice Scalia called it "the prototypical case involving the triumph of supposed 'legislative intent' . . . over the text of the law."[136] The scholar Philip Frickey joked that he advised his students that "*Holy Trinity Church* is the case you always cite when the text is hopelessly against you."[137]

Similarly, in *United Steelworkers v. Weber* (1979)[138] the Court relied on legislative history to uphold an affirmative action plan despite the statute's apparently clear language. In his dissent, Chief Justice Warren Burger accused his colleagues of "'amending' the statute to do precisely what both its sponsors and its opponents agreed the statute was not intended to do . . . effectively [rewriting the statute] [u]nder the guise of statutory 'construction.'"[139] He criticized the majority for using purpose to override text:

> Oddly, the Court seizes upon the very clarity of the statute almost as a justification for evading the unavoidable impact of its language. The Court blandly tells us that Congress could not really have meant what it said, for a "literal construction" would defeat the "purpose" of the statute—at least the congressional "purpose" as five Justices divine it today.[140]

---

136 Antonin Scalia, "Common Law Courts in a Civil-Law System: The Role of the United States Federal Courts in Interpreting the Constitution and Laws," in Antonin Scalia, *A Matter of Interpretation: Federal Courts and the Law*, pp. 18-23 (1997).

137 Philip P. "Frickey, From the Big Sleep to the Big Heat: The Revival of Theory in Statutory Interpretation," 77 *Minn. L. Rev.* 241, 247 (1992).

138 *United Steelworkers of Am., AFL-CIO-CLC v. Weber*, 443 U.S. 193 (1979).

139 *Id.* at 216 (dissenting, C. J. Burger).

140 *Id.* at 217 (dissenting, C. J. Burger).

He then posed the central interpretive question: "But how are judges supposed to ascertain the purpose of a statute except through the words Congress used and the legislative history of the statute's evolution?"[141] Chief Justice Burger's use of the conjunctive—"and"—begs the question: how should judges decide when the words appear to conflict with the legislative history?

That question becomes even more compelling when applied to constitutional amendments, where the operative text is ratified by numerous state legislatures and can be altered only through Article V's deliberately rigorous process. For that reason, courts have been more hesitant to depart from constitutional text than from statutory language. This principle was reaffirmed by *United States v. Sprague* (1931), where the Court rejected purpose-based arguments in light of clear constitutional text, stating that: "[w]here the intention is clear, there is no room for construction and no excuse for interpolation or addition."[142] Yet this formulation begs the question: how should courts proceed when "the intention is clear" *and* conflicts with the equally clear text?

Applying these principles to the 22nd Amendment, the text is not ambiguous. The word "elected" in the 22nd Amendment is functionally different from the words "shall become president" in the 25th Amendment. It is also different from the words "shall devolve," which, in Article 2, Section 1, Clause 6, describe how the vice president or other officials become president "in case of the removal of the president. . . ." It is also different, though perhaps a bit closer, to the words of the 12th Amendment determining what happens if the presidential electors were to fail to elect a president by a majority: "the

141 *Id.*

142 *United States v. Sprague*, 282 U.S. 716, 731 (1931).

House of Representatives shall choose immediately, by ballot, the President," with each state casting one vote.[143] The words "by ballot" suggest that the process of choosing could be considered a form of election. But that too is not clear beyond dispute.

Courts have consistently recognized this distinction. At the time of drafting and adoption of the 22nd Amendment—and in subsequent cases—federal courts have treated "elected" as referring strictly to accession through popular vote, declining to extend the term to appointments, succession, or other lawful mechanisms for assuming office. Although the Supreme Court has never addressed whether a twice-elected president could serve again through non-electoral means, it has acknowledged in analogous cases[144] that officials may assume office through appointment or legislative selection, and that such methods do not constitute "elections." Federal courts across the country have recognized the same principle appears in vacancy and succession cases involving US senators,[145] which confirmed that interim appointments do not constitute "elections."

To complicate matters even further, electors—under Article 2—are appointed, "in such a manner as the legislator may direct. . . ." In other words, a state legislature may decide to "appoint"—not "elect"—the electors who then determine who shall become president. This was not changed by the 12th Amendment. Accordingly, at the time of the adoption of the original Constitution and the first 12th Amendments, a person

143 The US Constitution is reprinted in the appendix.

144 *Fortson v. Morris*, 385 U.S. 231 (1966); *Sailors v. Board of Education*, 387 U.S. 105 (1967): *Rodriguez v. Popular Democratic Party*, 457 U.S.1 (1982).

145 *Valenti v. Rockefeller*, 292 F. Supp. 851 (S.D.N.Y. 1968) (involving Senator Robert Kennedy), *Trinsey v. Pennsylvania*, 941 F.2d 224 (3d Cir. 1991) (involving Senator John Heinz), and *Judge v. Quinn*, 612 F.3d 537 (7th Cir. 2010) (involving Senator Obama).

could have become president without there having been *any election*! All the electors could have been appointed, and they then could have chosen him to be president. This is not what has ever happened, but the Constitution, as understood at the time, would not have precluded such a non-election process. Indeed, the antagonism many among the Founders Fathers had toward "democracy" and the widespread use of the term "republic" suggests that the electoral college itself was not designed to promote "elections" as we now understand that term of democracy.

Despite the fact that the Constitution and the 12th Amendment do not explicitly require that the electors, who "vote by ballot" for who shall be president, must themselves be elected, rather than appointed, the 22nd Amendment uses the term "elected." By the time that amendment became part of the Constitution, all the states elected, rather than appointed, their electors. The popular understanding of the word "elected" included chosen by electors, regardless of how the electors themselves were selected. Thus, the 22nd Amendment could aptly describe the process as being "elected to the office of the President," and could mandate that "no person shall be <u>elected</u> to the office of the President more than twice . . ."

Purposivists acknowledge that a strict textual reading may produce an absurd result—for example, denying birthright citizenships to children of US citizens serving abroad. By the same reasoning, they may concede that the word "elected" is linguistically precise, yet argue that a rigid interpretation could frustrate the amendment's underlying purpose: to limit extended presidential tenure in the aftermath of FDR's four terms. Those who take this view contend that "elected" should be read functionally to cover *any* accession to the presidency resulting in continued service, and that the narrower term reflected drafting compromise rather than substantive design, a position borne out by the legislative history of the 22nd Amendment

Ultimately, textualists contend that the amendment's unambiguous language must be dispositive unless literal application would yield absurd results (however that term is defined). Purposivists counter that the amendment's structural purpose—to limit extended presidential service—could be undermined if succession allows a third term, even if technically permissible under the amendment's wording, particularly the operative term "elected."

The bottom line is that Congress deliberately rejected broad and all-encompassing language that would have unequivocally prohibited a two-term president from again serving, acting, or holding the office of president in favor of narrow language that only prohibits him from being elected to that office for a third term. They made this textual decision deliberately as part of a compromise that enabled quick resolution of disputes over language. Part of the claimed reason for this deliberate decision was to simplify and clarify the language so as to make its intentions more obvious to average Americans. To the extent that this explains the changes in the text, it supports paying serious attention to the precise words finally agreed upon as part of the compromise. It is certainly a strong argument against accepting textual formulations that were *expressly rejected* as part of the compromise process. Thus, under long-held principles of constitutional construction, the amendment should not be rewritten to prohibit a two-term president from becoming "ineligible to *hold* the office of President, under any and all circumstances and contingencies."[146]

This approach aligns with the Supreme Court's own

---

146 The Jan. 3 and Feb 5. 1947 drafts of House Joint Resolution 27 included that language, see, *supra* Chapter 3.

interpretive method.[147] The Court has repeatedly held that changes in statutory language reflect changes in meaning. As it explained on numerous occasions, "it will not assume that Congress intended 'to enact statutory language that it has earlier discarded in favor of other language.'"[148] In *Russello v. United States*, the Court observed: "Where Congress includes limiting language in an earlier draft of a bill but deletes it prior to enactment, it may be presumed that the limitation was not intended."[149]

To be sure, these interpretive methods are presumptive rather than conclusive, but that surely shifts the burden onto those who advocate purposivist interpretations to overcome the general rule that Congress meant precisely what it finally wrote—and not what it expressly chose to omit.

Resolving the tension between a textual and purposivist reading depends on whether the text is deemed sufficiently clear to control despite countervailing evidence of the amendment's purpose, or whether the drafting history and broader context reasonably support interpreting "elected" as implicitly encompassing other means of accession to the presidency.

Even if textual analysis suggests a narrow prohibition, permitting a former two-term president to serve again—whether through statutory succession or other non-electoral mechanisms—raises distinct questions about democratic expectations, constitutional stability, and the appropriate role of courts versus political branches. These concerns extend interpretive methodology. They reflect what my late

---

147 See Dan Coenen, *supra* n.89 at p. 1299.

148 *Chickasaw Nation v. United States*, 534 U.S. 84, 93 (2001) (citing *INS v. Cardoza—Fonseca*, 480 U.S. 421, 443 (1987) and quoting *Nachman Corp. v. Pension Benefit Guaranty Corporation*, 446 U.S. 359, 392–393 (1980)); *Gulf Oil Corp. v. Copp Paving Co.*, 419 U.S. 186, 200 (1974).

149 464 U.S. 16, 23–24 (1983).

colleague Ronald Dworkin referred to as a "moral reading" of the Constitution[150]—an approach that recognizes that constitutional interpretation necessarily engages moral and political principles and cannot rely exclusively on historical intent or literal text.

Viewed in this light, the inquiry is not exhausted by interpretive methodology alone. It instead gives rise to a set of related structural and normative questions, including the following:

1. In light of the fact that the Constitution provides several mechanisms for becoming and serving as president <u>other</u> than being elected, does the word "elected" prohibit a two-term president from serving a third term to which he was not "elected," but which he achieved by one of those other mechanisms?
2. In light of these alternative mechanisms, which were well known by the framers of the 22nd Amendment, why did they write the amendment to prohibit a two-term president from being "elected" to a third term when they easily could have borrowed more inclusive terms—such as "become," "act," "serve," "be appointed," "devolve," or "assume by any means"—that would have been clear, definitive, and unambiguous?
3. In light of these textual and purposive questions, should the 22nd Amendment be interpreted to prohibit a two-term president from serving a third time if he achieves that office without being elected?
4. Is the answer to the last question sufficiently clear to warrant the courts to remove a president who claims the office by means other than election? Or would that be a "political question" that the judicial branch should abstain from deciding?

---

150 Ronald Dworkin, *Freedom's Law* (1996).

The next chapter therefore turns to the moral and policy-based arguments against endorsing such a third-term pathway. It asks whether exceptional circumstances might justify a different outcome or whether such questions are ultimately better left to the political process—including a clarifying amendment—rather than the courts.

PART IV
THE POLICY ARGUMENTS AGAINST A THIRD-TERM PRESIDENT

★ ★ ★

In today's highly polarized political environment, separating the abstract constitutional question of whether a two-term president could ever serve again from current debates about President Trump is no easy task. The analysis that follows aims to consider the question in principle, rather than as a judgment about any particular president.

Over the course of my career, I have worked with political actors across the political spectrum. I represented President Trump in his first impeachment, but I also consulted with President Clinton's legal team in his impeachment. I have defended several Democratic political figures including Senators Ted Kennedy and Alan Cranston, as well as a number of national and local political figures. I am no longer a "member"—whatever that means—of the Democratic Party, largely because of its weakening support for Israel. But nor have I joined the Republican Party, largely because of its positions on domestic issues that are important to me. I now consider myself an independent politically. More broadly, I am a constitutional libertarian, meritocratic egalitarian, and constructive contrarian.

I have a long history of constitutional non-partisanship and my legal conclusions have angered both sides. I have strong views on many issues, which I often express in strong terms. But I have rarely been accused of pandering to any party in articulating my constitutional position. My strongest views relate to freedom of speech and due process, as well as the security of Israel and the Jewish people, but those are unlikely to bear directly on the abstract constitutional questions raised by the 22nd Amendment.

I began this inquiry without certainty where the research would take me, though my initial instinct was that it would come out against a two-term president being able to serve a third term. That was my personal preference, but preferences do not—at least on the conscious level—determine my constitutional conclusions.

Readers may of course, quarrel with my claims of neutrality and disagree with the conclusions reached here. The relevant question is whether the research, analysis, and reasoning withstand scrutiny on their own terms. With these considerations in mind, let us move from legal to policy analysis.

Chapter 8

Are There No Circumstances in Which a Two-Term President Should Serve a Third Term?

★ ★ ★

The issue of whether a two-term president could or ever should serve a third term can best be considered by testing a hypothetical situation—a thought experiment—such as the ones I frequently presented to my students when I taught at Harvard for half a century:

The nation is at war, suffering from a depression and afflicted with a lethal pandemic. During this perfect storm of disasters, both the president and vice president are assassinated. A sixty-year-old former two-term president is serving as Speaker of the House. He is extremely popular with voters from both parties because of his successful bipartisan efforts to solve previous perfect storms. Voters from both parties want to see him in the Oval Office. He wants to serve. There are not enough votes to amend the Constitution. Should the 22nd Amendment preclude him from being appointed president under the statutory succession provisions?

In presenting this hypothetical, I deliberately hide the party and name of the two-term president so as not to let the abstract answer be influenced by partisan or personal considerations. In the real world, of course, we would want to know the identities and party affiliations of all the actors. If the questions were "Should Trump, Obama, Clinton, or Bush be allowed to run for a third term?" the answer for most people would depend, at least in part, on who the two-term president was. By denying that information, I create a veil of ignorance—such as that advocated by the philosopher John Rawls[151]—that makes it harder for partisan or personal preferences to influence the answer to my abstract question.

So putting aside (if possible) the question of whether Donald Trump should be allowed to serve a third term, what is the most correct (or least incorrect) answer to the following abstract question: in light of the final text, the preliminary texts rejected in the name of compromise, and the relatively clear purpose of the 22nd Amendment, are there any circumstances, even if extreme, under which a two-term president should be constitutionally permitted to serve a third term to which he has not been elected? I am confident that for many of my more partisan academic colleagues the answer would depend on *who* that person was. That is why I constructed the hypothetical with a mandatory blindness to that fact.

In a democracy, the ultimate check on abuse of power is the electorate. Though FDR was elected for a third and fourth term, his margins of victory were considerably smaller than

151 John Rawls described his veil of ignorance as a "situation [in which] no one knows his place in society, his class position or social status, nor does anyone know his fortune in the distribution of natural assets and abilities, his intelligence, strength, and the like." John Rawls, A *Theory of Justice*, p. 11 (1971) (Revised edition, 2009).

for his first two terms.[152] There is reason to believe that these reduced margins were attributable, at least in part, to opposition to his breaking the two-term tradition.[153] There is even better reason to believe that there would be more opposition to an attempt to circumvent the intent, even if not the text, of the 22nd Amendment.

If, as Justice Louis Brandeis observed, states are our "laboratories of democracy,"[154] it is instructive to examine how they approached term limits. Thirty-seven states impose some form of term limits on governors. Of those, only ten states adopt lifetime limits of two terms—similar to the 22th Amendment—while the majority instead bar more than two consecutive terms.

Many governors have circumvented these term limits by serving non-consecutive terms. Notably, Governor George Wallace of Alabama had his wife elected governor to avoid the ban on consecutive terms, openly treating her as a figurehead while continuing to direct policy; he was later reelected to a third non-consecutive term, adhering to the letter—if not the spirit—of the state constitution. Others returned after extended absences, such as Cecil Underwood of West Virginia, who served from 1957–1961 and again from 1996–2001.

By contrast, the drafters of the 22nd Amendment—who, unlike the original Framers were writing at a time when longer life expectancy made multiple non-consecutive terms

---

152 While FDR won in 1932 and 1936 with margins of almost 18 percent and 25 percent, he won the 1940 and 1944 elections with less than a 10 percent margin.

153 In fact, between 1940 and 1943 eight states passed resolutions calling for presidential term limits, including FDR's home state of New York.

154 *New State Ice Co. v. Liebmann*, 285 U.S. 262, 311 (1932).

plausible—could have adopted a consecutive-term model.[155] Instead, they chose language that unequivocally bars a twice-elected president from ever being elected again, whether consecutively or nonconsecutively.

The legislative history offers little clarity as to why nonconsecutive service was categorically excluded, even after a prolonged hiatus. If, however, the amendment was primarily intended to prevent another prolonged FDR-style presidency, one may infer that the drafters were focused less on the possibility of a former twice-elected president with a late-career comeback focused on preventing a scenario in which a president could alternate terms with a politically aligned successor in order to circumvent term limits and to retain power.

In this light, the amendment may be understood as deliberately overinclusive in respect to nonconsecutive terms, to foreclose even low-probability strategies that might enable a former president to retain long-term influence over national policy and executive power through tactics such as those employed by Governor Wallace.[156]

The risks of an unlimited presidential term are considerably higher for a president than for a governor. Many states have recall mechanisms—entirely absent at the federal system—and

---

155 Bill Clinton appeared sympathetic to a system limiting presidents to two consecutive terms rather than a lifetime cap. Clinton was only fifty-four when he left office and said that he would have considered running for a third term but for the 22nd Amendment. In a 2000 *Rolling Stone* interview, Clinton suggested that rising life expectancy may have rendered the 22nd Amendment unnecessarily restrictive and argued that it should be amended to limit a president to two consecutive terms. Jann S. Werner, "Bill Clinton: The *Rolling Stone* Interview," Dec. 28, 2000.

156 As a textual matter, the Constitution does not impose term limits on the vice presidency. So in theory, this leaves open the possibility that an individual with durable control over a political party could serve repeatedly as vice president, while successive presidents function largely as nominal heads of the executive branch.

impeaching a governor is generally easier than impeaching a president.

In this respect US states resemble parliamentary democracies, such as Germany and Israel, where political leaders have been able to remain in office for long periods without strict term limits. In Germany, Helmut Kohl and Angela Merkel each served as chancellor for sixteen years. In Israel, David Ben Gurion served a total of fourteen years, and Benjamin Netanyahu has served more than sixteen years across multiple non-consecutive terms. In parliamentary systems, leaders can be removed at any time through mechanisms such as a vote of no confidence. The US federal system of government is a presidential system in which a sitting president may be ousted only through the far more onerous procedures of invocation of the 25th Amendment or impeachment.[157]

As comparative politics scholar Juan Linz has noted, presidential systems have historically been more susceptible to democratic erosion.[158] This may help to explain why the abolition of presidential term limits may carry greater risks in the United States than in parliamentary systems such as those of Germany or Israel.

---

157 I was involved in both the Clinton and Trump impeachments. See Alan M. Dershowitz, *Sexual McCarthyism: Clinton, Starr, and the Emerging Constitutional Crisis* (1999) and Alan M. Dershowitz, *Defending the Constitution* (2000).

158 For the seminal analysis on this issue, see Juan J. Linz, "The Perils of Presidentialism," *Journal of Democracy* Vol. 1, no. 1 (Winter 1990), pp. 51–69.

Chapter 9

Presidential Incapacity and the Vice Presidency

★ ★ ★

Presidential systems face a distinctive structural risk: executive stability depends on both the president and the vice president. Unlike parliamentary systems, which can replace leaders swiftly through a vote of no confidence, the United States relies on impeachment or the 25th Amendment—mechanisms that are intentionally difficult to invoke. In this context, it is critical to recall that the vice president is not merely ceremonial but, as Judge Richard Posner observed, a "*contingent president*"[159]—or, more colloquially, only one heartbeat away from the presidency. Despite its constitutional significance, the vice presidency has historically been treated as a political afterthought, often marginal to policymaking and selected primarily for electoral considerations—famously satirized in HBO's *Veep*. This reality weakens one of the Constitution's few mechanisms designed for ensuring continuity in the event of presidential incapacity or death.

---

159 See discussion *infra*, p. 57.

Franklin D. Roosevelt justified seeking a third term by pointing to extraordinary wartime conditions that required continuity of leadership.[160] Yet he selected a vice president who would not likely have provided that in the event of his death. Indeed, he replaced Henry Wallace when he ran for a fourth term and selected a relatively obscure senator, Harry S. Truman, who in retrospect provided such continuity, but who at the time did not seem to. Roosevelt's continuity-based argument would have been more persuasive had he selected vice presidents for their capacity as credible successors, rather than on their short-term perceived electoral benefits.

In a democracy, no one is indispensable—not even the president. For that reason, the president has a responsibility to pick a vice president who is capable of assuming office, whether temporarily or permanently. Unlike Congress or the Supreme Court, the presidency is never in recess; it is continuous. The Founders—who drafted the Constitution before the rise of organized political parties and the modern practice of electoral ticket-balancing—assumed that the vice president would be chosen for qualifications comparable to those of the president, precisely because he might be required at any moment to assume the powers and duties of the office. As Hamilton wrote in *The Federalist Papers*, "as the Vice-President may occasionally become a substitute for the president . . . all the reasons which recommend the mode of election prescribed for the one apply with great if not with equal force to the manner of appointing the other."[161]

---

160 President Trump, for example, has invoked his own indispensability ("I alone can fix it.") and has even jokingly suggested remaining in office "for at least 10 or 14 years." Felicia Sonmez, "Trump Again Jokes About Staying on as President for More than Two Terms," *Washington Post*, April 18, 2019.

161 *Federalist Papers*, No. 68 "The Mode of Electing the President" (March 14, 1788), available at https://avalon.law.yale.edu/18th_century/fed68.asp.

This issue has received public scrutiny on several occasions. John McCain's selection of Sarah Palin in 2008 prompted widespread concern due to McCain's age (seventy-two) and medical history, highlighting the possibility that an inexperienced running mate might assume the presidency. The concern was not hypothetical. In 1991, shortly after the Gulf War, President George H. W. Bush was hospitalized with atrial fibrillation. Preparations were made to transfer power under Section 3 of the 25th Amendment to Vice President Dan Quayle—whose readiness was widely questioned—though the procedure was ultimately avoided.[162] It was one of the rare moments when presidential disability protocols were seriously contemplated in wartime.

History offers even more dramatic examples. After President Woodrow Wilson's debilitating stroke in 1919, his wife and physician effectively managed presidential affairs for over a year.[163] Ronald Reagan was diagnosed with Alzheimer's disease five years after leaving office. Although no contemporaneous diagnosis was made, Reagan's own son later suggested that symptoms may have been present during his presidency.[164] And, according to some accounts, President Biden's late-term cognitive decline in 2024 significantly affected some of his policy actions (and inactions) before he ultimately withdrew from the race.[165]

Such episodes demonstrate that presidential incapacity is neither theoretical nor infrequent. Posner is therefore correct:

---

162 See, e.g., "President Dan Quayle? Yes, It Almost Happened, for a Few Hours Back in 1991," Reuters, Dec. 6, 2011.

163 Howard Markel, "When a Secret President Ran the Country," PBS, Oct. 2, 2015.

164 Ed Pilkington, "Ronald Reagan Had Alzheimer's While President, Says Son," *The Guardian*, Jan. 17, 2011.

165 Jake Tapper and Alex Thompson, *Original Sin* (2025).

in electing a vice president, we also elect a potential president. Yet under Franklin Roosevelt—until the selection of Harry S. Truman in 1944—the vice presidency remained largely inconsequential. Who served as vice president during FDR's first two terms? Exactly.[166]

This historical neglect underscores why, in a presidential system with limited removal mechanisms, greater vigilance is required in selecting those who may be called upon to assume the presidency.

Here is an imperfect but perhaps useful analogy: the vice president is a bit like a child's godparent. The role is mostly ceremonial—until it suddenly isn't. A godparent is rarely expected to step in, but if something happens to the parent, they must be ready to take full responsibility. Ideally, a godparent is chosen based on their ability to care for the child if the worst were to occur. In practice, though, godparents are often picked for symbolic or relational reasons, not because they are truly qualified to step in as guardians.

The same is often true of the vice presidency. Running mates are frequently selected based on factors such as geographic balance or other electoral advantage rather than their readiness to govern. Yet the vice president is, in Richard Posner's phrase, a "contingent president"—one heartbeat away from the office. And the risk becomes greater, not lesser, if he becomes president for an extended or extraordinary time.

---

166 Answer: John Nance Garner, who was vice president from 1933–1941 and not seen as a viable successor in the event of presidential incapacity.

Chapter 10

Would the Supreme Court Review an Unelected President Serving a Third Term, and If So How Would It Decide?

★ ★ ★

If any serious effort were to be made by any two-term president to seek a third term, it is clear that the judicial branch would become involved. What is not clear is the timing and substance of any such involvement and whether the Supreme Court would ultimately decide the constitutional issue at stake.

There are many possible scenarios—some more likely than others—in which the Supreme Court might be asked to decide whether a two-term president could lawfully serve a third term. If a two-term president were to decide to run for vice president, announcing that he intended to arrange for the president to resign so that he could be elevated to the presidency—the Steve Bannon scenario—a lawsuit could be brought by his opponent and perhaps others who might claim standing to object to this clear effort to circumvent the 22nd Amendment. In addition to the circumvention argument, his qualifications to run for vice president could be challenged under the 12th

Amendment which provides that "no person constitutionally ineligible to the office of President shall be eligible to that of Vice-President of the United States."

Other scenarios would involve an election of a president and vice president both of whom decide to resign so that the two-term president who was in line of succession could ascend to the presidency.[167] Such an ascension could be challenged under the 22nd Amendment and the relevant statutes.

Yet other scenarios, discussed earlier, could result in judicial challenges in the lower courts and eventually in the Supreme Court.

---

167 This scenario was suggested by Professor James Sample. In an email to the *Wall Street Journal*, he wrote "[t]he one scenario about which I think there is quasi-credible concern is a scenario in which two allies—perhaps JD Vance and Donald Trump Jr. or whomever, run with a plan not to serve; resign upon taking office; and because the Speaker of the House is not required to be a Member of Congress, Trump is elected Speaker, with the aim of succession." Brian Schwartz, "Trump Told by Alan Dershowitz Constitutionality of Third Term Is Unclear," Dec. 17, 2025.

Chapter 11

How the Supreme Court Might Review the Issue

★ ★ ★

There is no guarantee that the High Court would take the case and decide it on the merits. There are reasons why the Supreme Court might agree or decline to hear such a case.

Chief Justice Roberts has described his judicial approach as that of a "minimalist"—one who seeks to decide no more than necessary to resolve the case before the Court. In his confirmation hearing, quoted in the preface, he likened his role to that of a baseball umpire, whose task is "to call balls and strikes" rather than rewrite the rulebook. This commitment to institutional restraint reflects his longstanding concern, shared by federal judges across the political and judicial spectrum, about preserving the court's legitimacy in an era when judicial decisions are increasingly perceived solely through partisan lenses. Consistent with this philosophy, Chief Justice Roberts routinely relies on constitutional avoidance and related doctrines to sidestep broader constitutional questions. He has consistently favored incremental change—an approach that some liberal academic critics of the Roberts Court have described as "death by a thousand cuts."[168]

As discussed earlier, the abstract question of whether a twice-elected president may lawfully serve a third term ought to be resolved under a "veil of ignorance," meaning the identity of the officeholder—whether Donald Trump, Barack Obama, or any other—should be legally irrelevant.

A constitutional prohibition should never turn on partisan affiliation or electoral advantage. Notably, some scholarly interpretations of the 22nd Amendment have varied over time. Consider Cornell's Michael Dorf, a commentator on the US Supreme Court. He has called the language of the 22nd Amendment a "drafting error"[169] to be ignored when it was President Trump who could benefit from it. Yet in 2000, when Al Gore considered Bill Clinton serving as vice president, Dorf endorsed the idea, arguing that the 22nd Amendment did not preclude it and accordingly that nominating a twice-elected president to be vice president would not violate the spirit of the Constitution.[170] Even Bill Clinton himself thought that it would.[171] Now that Donald Trump might benefit from

---

168 See, e.g., Noah Feldman, "Voting Rights Are Dying by a Thousand Cuts," Bloomberg Opinion, August 8, 2024. ("[T]he most probable explanation for why both the Shelby County case and subsequent decisions chipping away at voting rights haven't triggered a public uproar is that Chief Justice John Roberts correctly calculated that it would be best to attack voting rights incrementally. . . . [U]nlike the court's more extreme conservatives, he prefers to make doctrinal changes slowly, one step at a time, to avoid undermining the court's legitimacy and creating backlash. That stealthy strategy has been depressingly effective when it comes to undercutting voting rights.")

169 Leo Sands, "Can Trump Run for a Third Term? The 22nd Amendment Flatly Prevents It," *Washington Post*, March 31, 2025.

170 Michael C. Dorf, "The Case for a Gore-Clinton Ticket," Findlaw, July 31, 2000, available at https://supreme.findlaw.com/legal-commentary/the-case-for-a-gore-clinton-ticket.htm.

171 Bill Clinton at the time also said "I don't believe I could do that. It would

his reading of the 22nd Amendment, Professor Dorf no longer agrees with this conclusion[172]—a convenient and partisan shift.[173]

Judges are not wholly immune from personal preferences and political influences either, as I argued in my 2001 book *Supreme Injustice*, a critique of the Court's decision in *Bush v. Gore*.[174] In that case, the conservative majority sacrificed legal consistency in what many viewed as an effort to achieve a politically desired outcome, a move that damaged the Court's credibility as an impartial tribunal. The reputational consequences of *Bush v. Gore* continue to cast a long shadow over the Court. Although the opinion purported to disclaim precedential value,[175] it *did* set a precedent in the court of public opinion. Polling reflects a steep decline in public confidence; according to recent data from Gallup, trust in the Supreme Court has fallen by nearly half since 2000.[176]

---

undermine the spirit of the Constitution." "Bill Clinton on Jimmy Kimmel: 'Most Days I Don't Miss' the White House," *The Washington Post*, April 3, 2014.

172 Before the 2024 election, Dorf explained his reassessment this way: "Imagine that Trump is elected to a second term this year and then decides to run again in 2028, this time with Vance heading the ticket and the expectation of a switcheroo after inauguration to give Trump a third term. . . . [A]lthough the specter of a third Trump term does not drive my reconsideration (though not exactly repudiation) of my 2000 view of the 22nd Amendment, it would be a beneficial side effect of rejecting it." Michael C. Dorf, "Could Former President Obama Run for Vice President?," July 22, 2024.

173 Michael C. Dorf, "A Third Trump Term?" DorfonLaw.org, Nov. 13, 2024. ("Citing the legislative history of the 22nd Amendment, my 2000 column also concluded that the switcheroo maneuver would not violate its spirit. On reflection, I now disagree with that conclusion.")

174 Alan M. Dershowitz: *Supreme Injustice* (2001).

175 The Court in *Bush v Gore* announced that "[o]ur consideration is limited to the present circumstances." *Bush v. Gore*, 531 U.S. 98, 109 (2000).

176 Jeffrey M. Jones, "Confidence in U.S. Supreme Court Sinks to Historic Low," June 23, 2022, available at https://news.gallup.com/poll/394103/confidence-supreme-court-sinks-historic-low.aspx (stating that only 25 percent of Americans have confidence in the Supreme Court compared to 50 percent in 2000).

While the Court still resolves most cases without partisan division,[177] 6–3 decisions are more common in the politically charged decisions. Few issues could be more politically fraught than whether a polarizing two-term president may lawfully seek a pathway to serving a third term.

The growing perception of judicial politicization is reflected in today's confirmation hearings.[178] Until relatively recently, Supreme Court nominees were confirmed by overwhelming bipartisan majorities. It is difficult to imagine today, but Justice Antonin Scalia was confirmed by a 98–0 vote! The Court was once viewed as standing above politics. As with many spheres that were once considered apolitical—sports, music, even science—the judiciary has become increasingly politicized. The *Bush v. Gore* decision accelerated, if not initiated,[179] this trend, and subsequent confirmation battles have further entrenched partisan expectation.[180]

This is to say that judges are (and perhaps always have

---

177 It should be noted that the vast majority of cases the Supreme Court decides to hear are not decided along partisan lines. For instance, in the 2024–25 term, only 9 percent of cases are split 6-3 along ideological lines. See Adam Feldman, "The 2024-2025 Supreme Court Term and the Roberts Court History," July 2, 2025, available at https://legalytics.substack.com/p/the-2024-2025-supreme-court-term.

178 Alan Dershowitz, *Confirming Justice – Or Injustice* (2020).

179 The modern politicization of Supreme Court confirmations is often traced to the 1987 nomination of Judge Robert H. Bork. The verb "to Bork" entered political vocabulary as shorthand for the organized derailing of a judicial nominee based on judicial philosophy rather than on personal or professional credentials.

180 Republican leaders who refused to hold hearings on Merrick Garland's nomination, asserting it was too late in the election cycle, later moved swiftly to confirm Justice Amy Coney Barrett under circumstances even closer to Election Day. Conversely, Democratic opposition to proposals to expand the Supreme Court gave way after the 2020 election to open discussion of expansion of the Court. Even judicial nominees have at times contributed to the perception of politicization. During his confirmation hearing, Justice Brett Kavanaugh stated that the opposition to his nomination seemed to be "revenge on behalf of the Clintons."

been) political actors—even if judging itself should never be partisan. This reality cannot be ignored when predicting how the Court would handle a case with profound implications for a presidential election.

If the identity of the former president were genuinely ignored—if the case were truly considered under a veil of ignorance—the Court would likely resolve it on narrow textual grounds. A majority could conclude that the 22nd Amendment prohibits only election, not service, such that a twice-elected president is not constitutionally disqualified from ascending to the presidency through non-electoral means. Justices Thomas, Gorsuch, Alito, and Barrett are strict textualists; Justices Kavanaugh and Roberts also adhere to textual interpretation, though with greater openness to pragmatic or institutional considerations.

In practice, though, any case would likely arise in the context of a specific president seeking a third term. Under those circumstances, the focus may shift from "What does the Constitution require?" to "What can the Supreme Court decide without inflicting further damage to its legitimacy—without risking another *Bush v. Gore*-style backlash?"

Chief Justice Roberts would be particularly attentive to this risk. Although conservative, he has, on occasion, provided pivotal votes to avoid the appearance or reality of partisanship—most notably in cases upholding the Affordable Care Act. His jurisprudence often reflects an effort to safeguard the Court as an institution. His voting record—siding with the majority in over 90 percent of the cases[181]—shows his attempt to be a moderating influence in a partisan era.

Much would depend on the precise nature and procedural

---

181 Adam Feldman, "How the 2024 Term Fits into the History of the Roberts Court," SCOTUSblog, July 9, 2025.

posture of the case, in which review is sought. For example, if the litigation were filed *before* the election, challenging the ability of a twice-elected president to appear on a vice-presidential ballot, the Court could evade the substantive constitutional question on several familiar grounds. It might rule that private voters lack standing because they cannot show a concrete, particularized harm distinct from that suffered by the electorate at large. A rival candidate may likewise be found to have only a generalized grievance rather than the direct injury required under the case or controversy requirements of Article III of the Constitution.[182] The Court could also conclude that the issue is not ripe for adjudication because no constitutional violation has yet occurred: the candidate has not assumed office, and any hypothetical future succession remains speculative.

If the challenge were to arise *after* the election, after the candidate has been declared vice president–elect, the Court might invoke the political question doctrine, holding that the Constitution commits the matter to Congress under the 12th Amendment. In such a scenario, Chief Justice Roberts and perhaps a majority might reason that determining whether an elected official is constitutionally eligible would improperly intrude upon prerogatives of the political branches.

A decision by the Supreme Court to *not* decide the case or the merits would have consequences no less serious than deciding the case. It would either leave conflicting lower-court decisions in place or leave unresolved the fundamental question of who is entitled to assume the presidency. As the late Justice Scalia wrote me in a personal letter several years after

---

182 In a recent decision, the Supreme Court held that political candidates have standing to challenge election laws "in advance of provable harm." See Ashley Lopez, "Candidates Have Legal Standing to Challenge Election Laws, the Supreme Court Rules," NPR, Jan. 14, 2026, https://www.npr.org/2026/01/14/nx-s1-5677318/supreme-court-bost-decision-candidate-standing.

Bush v. Gore, there were "severe time constraints" and "pressure" to come to a decision.[183] The constraints and pressures would exist in any case in which the presidency itself is subject to judicial determination.

The justices might, perhaps with considerable reluctance and appreciation of the institutional risks, vote to consider the case on the merits, and decide it on the narrowest reasonable grounds.

To paraphrase Yogi Berra: predicting Supreme Court decisions is difficult, especially future ones. It is particularly difficult, without knowing more about the factual context, to anticipate whether the Court would construe the 22nd Amendment textually and narrowly to permit a two-term president from serving a third term to which he was not elected. Much would depend on the precise non-elective route that brought him to the presidency.

For example, if it were the Bannon route—a deliberate advance plan to circumvent the 22nd Amendment by having the two-term president run for vice president with the express agreement of the presidential candidate to step aside—the High Court might well view that planned circumvention more negatively than a succession that was unplanned and brought about by unanticipated circumstances.

Consider, for example, the scenario I suggested earlier: The president and vice president are both assassinated and no one in the order of succession is deemed qualified or acceptable to the public to serve as president during a period of crisis.

---

183 Justice Scalia ended his lengthy letter with the following "P.S.: You may yet conclude that originalism is the safest course." The letter is also a reminder of a different time in constitutional discourse—one in which scholars could argue bitterly about first principles, yet remain friends. Even after ascending to the bench, Justice Scalia never ceased to think and write as a scholar, engaging competing arguments seriously and relishing rigorous intellectual debate.

This is not out of the question because the current statutory line of succession is riddled with design flaws. President Harry Truman—acutely aware that he had assumed office without ever being elected to the presidency—favored placing the Speaker of the House next in line after the vice president, precisely because the Speaker is an elected official.[184] But this solution raises two key problems. First, the Speaker often has no relevant executive or foreign policy experience. Second, the Speaker may belong to a different political party from the president, potentially triggering a partisan shift in the midst of a national crisis.

Even apart from these concerns, the statutory order of succession is structurally flawed because it prioritizes successors based on institutional seniority—how long each department has existed—rather than on competencies relevant to modern governance. This produces absurd results: the Secretary of Homeland Security, whose portfolio includes terrorism and national security threats, is last in line, well below the Secretaries of Agriculture or Transportation, whose portfolios do not include terrorism or national security threats (See table in appendix).

This has led some scholars to ask whether, in a moment of genuine constitutional or national crisis, it might not be preferable to allow a former president (even a twice-elected

---

184 It has been suggested that Truman's strained relationship with the president pro tempore influenced his decision to place the Speaker of the House ahead of the president pro tempore in the statutory line of succession. As the United States Senate website explains, "[s]ince one could make the same argument [about an elected representative] for the president pro tempore, Truman's decision may have reflected his strained relations with 78-year-old President Pro Tempore Kenneth McKellar and his warm friendship with 65-year-old House Speaker Sam Rayburn. After all, it was in Rayburn's hideaway office, where he had gone for a late afternoon glass of bourbon, that Truman first learned of his own elevation to the presidency." Presidential Succession Act, July 18, 1947, available at https://www.senate.gov/about/officers-staff/president-pro-tempore/presidential-succession-act.htm.

president)—someone with direct experience handling the office—to return to leadership if no alternative is immediately available or qualified.[185]

In that situation, if a former two-term president were to be a widely accepted—including on a bipartisan basis—and were chosen Speaker of the House as a pathway to the presidency, the Court might be more likely to defer to the House of Representatives rather than intervene. Other scenarios would likely present different outcomes in a real-world crisis. A two-term president seeking a third term by any means would do so under substantial judicial uncertainty. This uncertainty, combined with other daunting considerations, might well deter any attempt to take such a controversial step.

---

185 See Richard Albert, "The Constitutional Politics of Presidential Succession," 39 *Hofstra L. Rev.* 497, 538 (2011).

Conclusion

My Answer to the Question Posed by the Title of the Book: Could President Trump Constitutionally Serve a Third Term?

★ ★ ★

As the back cover of this book cautions, readers seeking certainty will likely be disappointed. The analysis offered here does not yield a resolution that will satisfy all sides. Those convinced that the Constitution clearly forbids a two-term president from ever serving again will find that conclusion less secure than they might assume; so too will those who believe the opposite is beyond dispute. What this book demonstrates, beyond serious disagreement, is that there are plausible and competing constitutional arguments on both sides. Neither position deserves to be characterized as "unthinkable." I have thought about them and attempted to present each as objectively as I would if I were conducting a law school seminar on these issues. My goal as a teacher was first to complexify issues that seem simple and then to simplify them as much as possible so that they can be understood by citizens. With that caveat, now to my answer.

The text alone—"shall be elected . . . more than twice"—does not explicitly preclude a third term to which the two-term president is not elected. The final text, *together* with *rejected* proposed texts—"chosen," "serve," "be eligible," "hold," "act"—strengthens that narrower view of the prohibition. So if the text and the specific legislative history that led to it are deemed dispositive, there are strong arguments in favor of a non-elected third term.

But if the broader legislative purpose is deemed dispositive, then an argument can be made for substituting (or adding) the rejected preliminary language to the accepted final language ("elected" really means "serve" etc.).

Finally, if the understanding of voters and citizens is to be considered, it seems clear that this understanding is that at two-term president is prohibited from serving a third term without regard to the manner or procedure by which he achieves that third term. The best proof of this understanding may be reflected in the words of President Trump himself: "If you read [the 22nd Amendment], it is pretty clear . . . I'm not allowed to run. It's too bad."[186] President Trump's personal understanding of the 22nd Amendment can serve as a logical transition point from the constitutional to the political—without necessarily becoming partisan.

A significant number of voters—including many who might otherwise support a two-term president like Trump—would likely view any attempt at return through the vice presidency as an end-run around the Constitution. That perceived circumvention would carry political costs that might significantly reduce the number of his previous supporters who would vote

186 See *supra* n.71 at p. 38.

for him a third term[187]—as it did with FDR, even before the 22nd Amendment.[188]

Whether Trump could succeed, if he chooses to try, would probably depend on a mix of law, reality, and politics. The calculus could change depending on the identity and perceived extremism or unacceptability of his opponent. To invoke a hypothetical: if Democrats were to nominate a candidate considered radically outside mainstream political views, such as AOC, a considerable number of voters might prioritize their political fears over their constitutional qualms, tolerating what they would otherwise view as a circumvention. It might also depend on the nature and degree of the crisis and the comparative ability of the other candidate to confront the dangers.

Thus, while objective constitutional analysis may provide an arguable theoretical pathway to a third term, political reality might well foreclose it. Perhaps James Madison was right after all: term limits should be more a matter of public choice than constitutional law.

Public choice should also determine the future of the 22nd Amendment. If the public overwhelmingly favors an absolute disqualification for any third-term president, regardless of circumstances, it should not be difficult or controversial to remedy the current uncertainty by amending it to prohibit any

---

187 As Prof. Coenen notes, "It is farfetched to think the nation's voters would fail to detect a self-serving effort to pull a Twenty-Second-Amendment fast one on them or to embrace with enthusiasm a Presidential ticket openly designed to circumvent the Constitution's strictures." Coenen, *supra* n.89, at 1313 n.138.

188 According to a recent poll, 58 percent of Republican voters would want Trump to run in 2028, yet they were less likely than Democrats to think that Trump would try do that given the 22nd Amendment. "Half of Voters Think Trump Will Try to Run Again—but a Strong Majority Don't Want Him To," Data For Progress, Aug. 27, 2025, available at https://www.dataforprogress.org/blog/2025/8/27/half-of-voters-think-trump-will-try-to-run-again-but-a-strong-majority-dont-want-him-to. I am skeptical of these polls.

two-term president from "serving as," "acting as," or "holding office of" president. It would be unlikely to see such a curative amendment ratified before the 2028 election, but it could probably be done in time for 2032.

On a more fundamental level, the survival and thriving of democracy ultimately depends on the passions of the citizens more than on the parchment promises on the documents—even documents as important as the Constitution and its Bill of Rights. As the great Judge Learned Hand cautioned at the end of World War II: "I often wonder whether we do not rest our hopes too much upon constitutions, upon laws and upon courts. These are false hopes; believe me, these are false hopes. Liberty lies in the hearts of men and women; when it dies there, no constitution, no law, no court can even do much to help it."[189]

I disagree with Judge Hand when he says that no constitution, laws, or courts "can even do much" to help prevent tyranny. These institutions of democracy and checks and balances can slow down the process so as to permit our better angels to prevail. But in the end, liberty does depend on the good will of the citizens themselves. It is my belief in the virtues of most Americans that makes me a cautious optimist about our future.

189 Judge Learned Hand, "The Spirit of Liberty," (1944), available at https://www.thefire.org/research-learn/spirit-liberty-speech-judge-learned-hand-1944.

APPENDIX

★ ★ ★

This book is designed to present the readers with all sides to their complex issue. Therefore, it is appropriate to provide the reader easy access to the most relevant primary documentation, so that readers can reach their own conclusions.

Primary Sources

The United States Constitution

- Bill of Rights
- Subsequent Amendments
- Previous Drafts of the 22nd Amendment

The Federalist Papers

- Federalist No. 68 – The Mode of Electing the President (Hamilton)
- Federalist No. 72 – The Same Subject Continued, and Re-Eligibility of the Executive Considered (Hamilton)

The Presidential Succession Act (1947)

Current Presidential Line of Succession (2026) As Per the Presidential Succession Act

Presidential Succession by Vice Presidents
Acting Presidents Under the 25th Amendment

THE UNITED STATES CONSTITUTION

★ ★ ★

We the People of the United States, in Order to form a more perfect Union, establish Justice, insure domestic Tranquility, provide for the common defence, promote the general Welfare, and secure the Blessings of Liberty to ourselves and our Posterity, do ordain and establish this Constitution for the United States of America.

Article. I.

Section. 1.

All legislative Powers herein granted shall be vested in a Congress of the United States, which shall consist of a Senate and House of Representatives.

Section. 2.

The House of Representatives shall be composed of Members chosen every second Year by the People of the several States, and the Electors in each State shall have the Qualifications requisite for Electors of the most numerous Branch of the State Legislature.

No Person shall be a Representative who shall not have attained to the Age of twenty five Years, and been seven Years a Citizen of the United States, and who shall not, when elected, be an Inhabitant of that State in which he shall be chosen.

Representatives and direct Taxes shall be apportioned among the several States which may be included within this Union, according to their respective Numbers, which shall be determined by adding to the whole Number of free Persons, including those bound to Service for a Term of Years, and excluding Indians not taxed, three fifths of all other Persons. The actual Enumeration shall be made within three Years after the first Meeting of the Congress of the United States, and within every subsequent Term of ten Years, in such Manner as they shall by Law direct. The Number of Representatives shall not exceed one for every thirty Thousand, but each State shall have at Least one Representative; and until such enumeration shall be made, the State of New Hampshire shall be entitled to chuse three, Massachusetts eight, Rhode-Island and Providence Plantations one, Connecticut five, New-York six, New Jersey four, Pennsylvania eight, Delaware one, Maryland six, Virginia ten, North Carolina five, South Carolina five, and Georgia three.

When vacancies happen in the Representation from any State, the Executive Authority thereof shall issue Writs of Election to fill such Vacancies.

The House of Representatives shall chuse their Speaker and other Officers; and shall have the sole Power of Impeachment.

Section. 3.

The Senate of the United States shall be composed of two Senators from each State, chosen by the Legislature thereof, for six Years; and each Senator shall have one Vote.

Immediately after they shall be assembled in Consequence of the first Election, they shall be divided as equally as may be into three Classes. The Seats of the Senators of the first Class shall be vacated at the Expiration of the second Year, of the second Class at the Expiration of the fourth Year, and of the third Class at the Expiration of the sixth Year, so that one third may be chosen every second Year; and if Vacancies happen by Resignation, or otherwise, during the Recess of the Legislature of any State, the Executive thereof may make temporary Appointments until the next Meeting of the Legislature, which shall then fill such Vacancies.

No Person shall be a Senator who shall not have attained to the Age of thirty Years, and been nine Years a Citizen of the United States, and who shall not, when elected, be an Inhabitant of that State for which he shall be chosen.

The Vice President of the United States shall be President of the Senate, but shall have no Vote, unless they be equally divided.

The Senate shall chuse their other Officers, and also a President pro tempore, in the Absence of the Vice President, or when he shall exercise the Office of President of the United States.

The Senate shall have the sole Power to try all Impeachments. When sitting for that Purpose, they shall be on Oath or Affirmation. When the President of the United States is tried, the Chief Justice shall preside: And no Person shall be convicted without the Concurrence of two thirds of the Members present.

Judgment in Cases of Impeachment shall not extend further than to removal from Office, and disqualification to hold and enjoy any Office of honor, Trust or Profit under the United States: but the Party convicted shall nevertheless be liable and subject to Indictment, Trial, Judgment and Punishment, according to Law.

Section. 4.
The Times, Places and Manner of holding Elections for Senators and Representatives, shall be prescribed in each State by the Legislature thereof; but the Congress may at any time by Law make or alter such Regulations, except as to the Places of chusing Senators.

The Congress shall assemble at least once in every Year, and such Meeting shall be on the first Monday in December, unless they shall by Law appoint a different Day.

Section. 5.
Each House shall be the Judge of the Elections, Returns and Qualifications of its own Members, and a Majority of each shall constitute a Quorum to do Business; but a smaller Number may adjourn from day to day, and may be authorized to compel the Attendance of absent Members, in such Manner, and under such Penalties as each House may provide.

Each House may determine the Rules of its Proceedings, punish its Members for disorderly Behaviour, and, with the Concurrence of two thirds, expel a Member.

Each House shall keep a Journal of its Proceedings, and from time to time publish the same, excepting such Parts as may in their Judgment require Secrecy; and the Yeas and Nays of the Members of either House on any question shall, at the Desire of one fifth of those Present, be entered on the Journal.

Neither House, during the Session of Congress, shall, without the Consent of the other, adjourn for more than three days, nor to any other Place than that in which the two Houses shall be sitting.

Section. 6.
The Senators and Representatives shall receive a Compensation for their Services, to be ascertained by Law, and paid out of the Treasury of the United States. They shall in all Cases, except Treason, Felony and Breach of the Peace, be privileged from Arrest during their Attendance at the Session of their respective Houses, and in going to and returning from the same; and for any Speech or Debate in either House, they shall not be questioned in any other Place.

No Senator or Representative shall, during the Time for which he was elected, be appointed to any civil Office under the Authority of the United States, which shall have been created, or the Emoluments whereof shall have been encreased during such time; and no Person holding any Office under the United States, shall be a Member of either House during his Continuance in Office.

Section. 7.

All Bills for raising Revenue shall originate in the House of Representatives; but the Senate may propose or concur with Amendments as on other Bills.

Every Bill which shall have passed the House of Representatives and the Senate, shall, before it become a Law, be presented to the President of the United States; If he approve he shall sign it, but if not he shall return it, with his Objections to that House in which it shall have originated, who shall enter the Objections at large on their Journal, and proceed to reconsider it. If after such Reconsideration two thirds of that House shall agree to pass the Bill, it shall be sent, together with the Objections, to the other House, by which it shall likewise be reconsidered, and if approved by two thirds of that House, it shall become a Law. But in all such Cases the Votes of both Houses shall be determined by yeas and Nays, and the Names of the Persons voting for and against the Bill shall be entered on the Journal of each House respectively. If any Bill shall not be returned by the President within ten Days (Sundays excepted) after it shall have been presented to him, the Same shall be a Law, in like Manner as if he had signed it, unless the Congress by their Adjournment prevent its Return, in which Case it shall not be a Law.

Every Order, Resolution, or Vote to which the Concurrence of the Senate and House of Representatives may be necessary (except on a question of Adjournment) shall be presented to the President of the United States; and before the Same shall take Effect, shall be approved by him, or being disapproved by him, shall be repassed by two thirds of the Senate and House of Representatives, according to the Rules and Limitations prescribed in the Case of a Bill.

Section. 8.
The Congress shall have Power

To lay and collect Taxes, Duties, Imposts and Excises, to pay the Debts and provide for the common Defence and general Welfare of the United States; but all Duties, Imposts and Excises shall be uniform throughout the United States;

To borrow Money on the credit of the United States;

To regulate Commerce with foreign Nations, and among the several States, and with the Indian Tribes;

To establish an uniform Rule of Naturalization, and uniform Laws on the subject of Bankruptcies throughout the United States;

To coin Money, regulate the Value thereof, and of foreign Coin, and fix the Standard of Weights and Measures;

To provide for the Punishment of counterfeiting the Securities and current Coin of the United States;

To establish Post Offices and post Roads;

To promote the Progress of Science and useful Arts, by securing for limited Times to Authors and Inventors the exclusive Right to their respective Writings and Discoveries;

To constitute Tribunals inferior to the supreme Court;

To define and punish Piracies and Felonies committed on the high Seas, and Offences against the Law of Nations;

To declare War, grant Letters of Marque and Reprisal, and make Rules concerning Captures on Land and Water;

To raise and support Armies, but no Appropriation of Money to that Use shall be for a longer Term than two Years;

To provide and maintain a Navy;

To make Rules for the Government and Regulation of the land and naval Forces;

To provide for calling forth the Militia to execute the Laws of the Union, suppress Insurrections and repel Invasions;

To provide for organizing, arming, and disciplining, the Militia, and for governing such Part of them as may be employed in the Service of the United States, reserving to the States respectively, the Appointment of the Officers, and the Authority of training the Militia according to the discipline prescribed by Congress;

To exercise exclusive Legislation in all Cases whatsoever, over such District (not exceeding ten Miles square) as may, by Cession of particular States, and the Acceptance of Congress, become the Seat of the Government of the United States, and to exercise like Authority over all Places purchased by the Consent of the Legislature of the State in which the Same shall be, for the Erection of Forts, Magazines, Arsenals, dock-Yards, and other needful Buildings;—And

To make all Laws which shall be necessary and proper for carrying into Execution the foregoing Powers, and all other Powers vested by this Constitution in the Government of the United States, or in any Department or Officer thereof.

Section. 9.

The Migration or Importation of such Persons as any of the States now existing shall think proper to admit, shall not be prohibited by the Congress prior to the Year one thousand eight hundred and eight, but a Tax or duty may be imposed on such Importation, not exceeding ten dollars for each Person.

The Privilege of the Writ of Habeas Corpus shall not be suspended, unless when in Cases of Rebellion or Invasion the public Safety may require it.

No Bill of Attainder or ex post facto Law shall be passed.

No Capitation, or other direct, Tax shall be laid, unless in Proportion to the Census or enumeration herein before directed to be taken.

No Tax or Duty shall be laid on Articles exported from any State.

No Preference shall be given by any Regulation of Commerce or Revenue to the Ports of one State over those of another: nor shall Vessels bound to, or from, one State, be obliged to enter, clear, or pay Duties in another.

No Money shall be drawn from the Treasury, but in Consequence of Appropriations made by Law; and a regular Statement and Account of the Receipts and Expenditures of all public Money shall be published from time to time.

No Title of Nobility shall be granted by the United States: And no Person holding any Office of Profit or Trust under them, shall, without the Consent of the Congress, accept of any present, Emolument, Office, or Title, of any kind whatever, from any King, Prince, or foreign State.

Section. 10.

No State shall enter into any Treaty, Alliance, or Confederation; grant Letters of Marque and Reprisal; coin Money; emit Bills of Credit; make any Thing but gold and silver Coin a Tender in Payment of Debts; pass any Bill of Attainder, ex post facto Law, or Law impairing the Obligation of Contracts, or grant any Title of Nobility.

No State shall, without the Consent of the Congress, lay any Imposts or Duties on Imports or Exports, except what may be absolutely necessary for executing it's inspection Laws: and the net Produce of all Duties and Imposts, laid by any State on Imports or Exports, shall be for the Use of the Treasury of the United States; and all such Laws shall be subject to the Revision and Controul of the Congress.

No State shall, without the Consent of Congress, lay any Duty of Tonnage, keep Troops, or Ships of War in time of Peace, enter into any Agreement or Compact with another State, or with a foreign Power, or engage in War, unless actually invaded, or in such imminent Danger as will not admit of delay.

Article. II.
Section. 1.
The executive Power shall be vested in a President of the United States of America. He shall hold his Office during the Term of four Years, and, together with the Vice President, chosen for the same Term, be elected, as follows

Each State shall appoint, in such Manner as the Legislature thereof may direct, a Number of Electors, equal to the whole Number of Senators and Representatives to which the State may be entitled in the Congress: but no Senator or Representative, or Person holding an Office of Trust or Profit under the United States, shall be appointed an Elector.

The Electors shall meet in their respective States, and vote by Ballot for two Persons, of whom one at least shall not be an Inhabitant of the same State with themselves. And they shall make a List of all the Persons voted for, and of the Number of Votes for each; which List they shall sign and certify, and transmit sealed to the Seat of the Government of the United States, directed to the President of the Senate. The President of the Senate shall, in the Presence of the Senate and House of Representatives, open all the Certificates, and the Votes shall then be counted. The Person having the greatest Number of Votes shall be the President, if such Number be a Majority of the whole Number of Electors appointed; and if there be more than one who have such Majority, and have an equal Number of Votes, then the House of Representatives shall immediately chuse by Ballot one of them for President; and if no Person have a Majority, then from the five highest on the List the said House shall in like Manner chuse the President. But in chusing the President, the Votes shall be taken by States, the

Representation from each State having one Vote; A quorum for this Purpose shall consist of a Member or Members from two thirds of the States, and a Majority of all the States shall be necessary to a Choice. In every Case, after the Choice of the President, the Person having the greatest Number of Votes of the Electors shall be the Vice President. But if there should remain two or more who have equal Votes, the Senate shall chuse from them by Ballot the Vice President.

The Congress may determine the Time of chusing the Electors, and the Day on which they shall give their Votes; which Day shall be the same throughout the United States.

No Person except a natural born Citizen, or a Citizen of the United States, at the time of the Adoption of this Constitution, shall be eligible to the Office of President; neither shall any Person be eligible to that Office who shall not have attained to the Age of thirty five Years, and been fourteen Years a Resident within the United States.

In Case of the Removal of the President from Office, or of his Death, Resignation, or Inability to discharge the Powers and Duties of the said Office, the Same shall devolve on the Vice President, and the Congress may by Law provide for the Case of Removal, Death, Resignation or Inability, both of the President and Vice President, declaring what Officer shall then act as President, and such Officer shall act accordingly, until the Disability be removed, or a President shall be elected.

The President shall, at stated Times, receive for his Services, a Compensation, which shall neither be encreased nor diminished during the Period for which he shall have been elected, and he shall not receive within that Period any other Emolument from the United States, or any of them.

Before he enter on the Execution of his Office, he shall take the following Oath or Affirmation:—"I do solemnly swear (or affirm) that I will faithfully execute the Office of President of the United States, and will to the best of my Ability, preserve, protect and defend the Constitution of the United States."

Section. 2.

The President shall be Commander in Chief of the Army and Navy of the United States, and of the Militia of the several States, when called into the actual Service of the United States; he may require the Opinion, in writing, of the principal Officer in each of the executive Departments, upon any Subject relating to the Duties of their respective Offices, and he shall have Power to grant Reprieves and Pardons for Offences against the United States, except in Cases of Impeachment.

He shall have Power, by and with the Advice and Consent of the Senate, to make Treaties, provided two thirds of the Senators present concur; and he shall nominate, and by and with the Advice and Consent of the Senate, shall appoint Ambassadors, other public Ministers and Consuls, Judges of the supreme Court, and all other Officers of the United States, whose Appointments are not herein otherwise provided for, and which shall be established by Law: but the Congress may by Law vest the Appointment of such inferior Officers, as they think proper, in the President alone, in the Courts of Law, or in the Heads of Departments.

The President shall have Power to fill up all Vacancies that may happen during the Recess of the Senate, by granting Commissions which shall expire at the End of their next Session.

Section. 3.

He shall from time to time give to the Congress Information of the State of the Union, and recommend to their Consideration such Measures as he shall judge necessary and expedient; he may, on extraordinary Occasions, convene both Houses, or either of them, and in Case of Disagreement between them, with Respect to the Time of Adjournment, he may adjourn them to such Time as he shall think proper; he shall receive Ambassadors and other public Ministers; he shall take Care that the Laws be faithfully executed, and shall Commission all the Officers of the United States.

Section. 4.

The President, Vice President and all civil Officers of the United States, shall be removed from Office on Impeachment for, and Conviction of, Treason, Bribery, or other high Crimes and Misdemeanors.

Article III.

Section. 1.

The judicial Power of the United States, shall be vested in one supreme Court, and in such inferior Courts as the Congress may from time to time ordain and establish. The Judges, both of the supreme and inferior Courts, shall hold their Offices during good Behaviour, and shall, at stated Times, receive for their Services, a Compensation, which shall not be diminished during their Continuance in Office.

Section. 2.

The judicial Power shall extend to all Cases, in Law and Equity, arising under this Constitution, the Laws of the United States, and Treaties made, or which shall be made, under their Authority;—to all Cases affecting Ambassadors, other public Ministers and Consuls;—to all Cases of admiralty and maritime Jurisdiction;—to Controversies to which the United States shall be a Party;—to Controversies between two or more States;—between a State and Citizens of another State,—between Citizens of different States,—between Citizens of the same State claiming Lands under Grants of different States, and between a State, or the Citizens thereof, and foreign States, Citizens or Subjects.

In all Cases affecting Ambassadors, other public Ministers and Consuls, and those in which a State shall be Party, the supreme Court shall have original Jurisdiction. In all the other Cases before mentioned, the supreme Court shall have appellate Jurisdiction, both as to Law and Fact, with such Exceptions, and under such Regulations as the Congress shall make.

The Trial of all Crimes, except in Cases of Impeachment, shall be by Jury; and such Trial shall be held in the State where the said Crimes shall have been committed; but when not committed within any State, the Trial shall be at such Place or Places as the Congress may by Law have directed.

Section. 3.

Treason against the United States, shall consist only in levying War against them, or in adhering to their Enemies, giving them Aid and Comfort. No Person shall be convicted of Treason unless on the Testimony of two Witnesses to the same overt Act, or on Confession in open Court.

The Congress shall have Power to declare the Punishment of Treason, but no Attainder of Treason shall work Corruption of Blood, or Forfeiture except during the Life of the Person attainted.

Article. IV.

Section. 1.

Full Faith and Credit shall be given in each State to the public Acts, Records, and judicial Proceedings of every other State. And the Congress may by general Laws prescribe the Manner in which such Acts, Records and Proceedings shall be proved, and the Effect thereof.

Section. 2.

The Citizens of each State shall be entitled to all Privileges and Immunities of Citizens in the several States.

A Person charged in any State with Treason, Felony, or other Crime, who shall flee from Justice, and be found in another State, shall on Demand of the executive Authority of the State from which he fled, be delivered up, to be removed to the State having Jurisdiction of the Crime.

No Person held to Service or Labour in one State, under the Laws thereof, escaping into another, shall, in Consequence of any Law or Regulation therein, be discharged from such Service or Labour, but shall be delivered up on Claim of the Party to whom such Service or Labour may be due.

Section. 3.

New States may be admitted by the Congress into this Union; but no new State shall be formed or erected within the

Jurisdiction of any other State; nor any State be formed by the Junction of two or more States, or Parts of States, without the Consent of the Legislatures of the States concerned as well as of the Congress.

The Congress shall have Power to dispose of and make all needful Rules and Regulations respecting the Territory or other Property belonging to the United States; and nothing in this Constitution shall be so construed as to Prejudice any Claims of the United States, or of any particular State.

Section. 4.
The United States shall guarantee to every State in this Union a Republican Form of Government, and shall protect each of them against Invasion; and on Application of the Legislature, or of the Executive (when the Legislature cannot be convened) against domestic Violence.

Article. V.
The Congress, whenever two thirds of both Houses shall deem it necessary, shall propose Amendments to this Constitution, or, on the Application of the Legislatures of two thirds of the several States, shall call a Convention for proposing Amendments, which, in either Case, shall be valid to all Intents and Purposes, as Part of this Constitution, when ratified by the Legislatures of three fourths of the several States, or by Conventions in three fourths thereof, as the one or the other Mode of Ratification may be proposed by the Congress; Provided that no Amendment which may be made prior to the Year One thousand eight hundred and eight shall in any Manner affect the first and fourth Clauses in the Ninth Section of the first Article; and that no State, without its Consent, shall be deprived of its equal Suffrage in the Senate.

Article. VI.

All Debts contracted and Engagements entered into, before the Adoption of this Constitution, shall be as valid against the United States under this Constitution, as under the Confederation.

This Constitution, and the Laws of the United States which shall be made in Pursuance thereof; and all Treaties made, or which shall be made, under the Authority of the United States, shall be the supreme Law of the Land; and the Judges in every State shall be bound thereby, any Thing in the Constitution or Laws of any State to the Contrary notwithstanding.

The Senators and Representatives before mentioned, and the Members of the several State Legislatures, and all executive and judicial Officers, both of the United States and of the several States, shall be bound by Oath or Affirmation, to support this Constitution; but no religious Test shall ever be required as a Qualification to any Office or public Trust under the United States.

Article. VII.

The Ratification of the Conventions of nine States, shall be sufficient for the Establishment of this Constitution between the States so ratifying the Same.

BILL OF RIGHTS

Amendment I (1791)
Congress shall make no law respecting an establishment of religion, or prohibiting the free exercise thereof; or abridging the freedom of speech, or of the press; or the right of the people peaceably to assemble, and to petition the Government for a redress of grievances.

Amendment II (1791)
A well regulated Militia, being necessary to the security of a free State, the right of the people to keep and bear Arms, shall not be infringed.

Amendment III (1791)
No Soldier shall, in time of peace be quartered in any house, without the consent of the Owner, nor in time of war, but in a manner to be prescribed by law.

Amendment IV (1791)
The right of the people to be secure in their persons, houses, papers, and effects, against unreasonable searches and seizures, shall not be violated, and no Warrants shall issue, but upon probable cause, supported by Oath or affirmation, and particularly describing the place to be searched, and the persons or things to be seized.

Amendment V (1791)
No person shall be held to answer for a capital, or otherwise infamous crime, unless on a presentment or indictment of a Grand Jury, except in cases arising in the land or naval forces, or in the Militia, when in actual service in time of War or public

danger; nor shall any person be subject for the same offence to be twice put in jeopardy of life or limb; nor shall be compelled in any criminal case to be a witness against himself, nor be deprived of life, liberty, or property, without due process of law; nor shall private property be taken for public use, without just compensation.

Amendment VI (1791)
In all criminal prosecutions, the accused shall enjoy the right to a speedy and public trial, by an impartial jury of the State and district wherein the crime shall have been committed, which district shall have been previously ascertained by law, and to be informed of the nature and cause of the accusation; to be confronted with the witnesses against him; to have compulsory process for obtaining witnesses in his favor, and to have the Assistance of Counsel for his defence.

Amendment VII (1791)
In Suits at common law, where the value in controversy shall exceed twenty dollars, the right of trial by jury shall be preserved, and no fact tried by a jury, shall be otherwise re-examined in any Court of the United States, than according to the rules of the common law.

Amendment VIII (1791)
Excessive bail shall not be required, nor excessive fines imposed, nor cruel and unusual punishments inflicted.

Amendment IX (1791)
The enumeration in the Constitution, of certain rights, shall not be construed to deny or disparage others retained by the people.

Amendment X (1791)
The powers not delegated to the United States by the Constitution, nor prohibited by it to the States, are reserved to the States respectively, or to the people.

SUBSEQUENT AMENDMENTS

Amendment XI (1795/1798)
The Judicial power of the United States shall not be construed to extend to any suit in law or equity, commenced or prosecuted against one of the United States by Citizens of another State, or by Citizens or Subjects of any Foreign State.

Amendment XII (1804)
The Electors shall meet in their respective states and vote by ballot for President and Vice-President, one of whom, at least, shall not be an inhabitant of the same state with themselves; they shall name in their ballots the person voted for as President, and in distinct ballots the person voted for as Vice-President, and they shall make distinct lists of all persons voted for as President, and of all persons voted for as Vice-President, and of the number of votes for each, which lists they shall sign and certify, and transmit sealed to the seat of the government of the United States, directed to the President of the Senate;—The President of the Senate shall, in the presence of the Senate and House of Representatives, open all the certificates and the votes shall then be counted;—The person having the greatest Number of votes for President, shall be the President, if such number be a majority of the whole number of Electors appointed; and if no person have such majority, then from the persons having the highest numbers not exceeding three on the list of those voted for as President, the House of Representatives shall choose immediately, by ballot, the

President. But in choosing the President, the votes shall be taken by states, the representation from each state having one vote; a quorum for this purpose shall consist of a member or members from two-thirds of the states, and a majority of all the states shall be necessary to a choice. And if the House of Representatives shall not choose a President whenever the right of choice shall devolve upon them, before the fourth day of March next following, then the Vice-President shall act as President, as in the case of the death or other constitutional disability of the President—The person having the greatest number of votes as Vice-President, shall be the Vice-President, if such number be a majority of the whole number of Electors appointed, and if no person have a majority, then from the two highest numbers on the list, the Senate shall choose the Vice-President; a quorum for the purpose shall consist of two-thirds of the whole number of Senators, and a majority of the whole number shall be necessary to a choice. But no person constitutionally ineligible to the office of President shall be eligible to that of Vice-President of the United States.

Amendment XIII (1865)
Section 1. Neither slavery nor involuntary servitude, except as a punishment for crime whereof the party shall have been duly convicted, shall exist within the United States, or any place subject to their jurisdiction.

Section 2. Congress shall have power to enforce this article by appropriate legislation.

Amendment XIV (1868)
Section 1. All persons born or naturalized in the United States, and subject to the jurisdiction thereof, are citizens of the United States and of the State wherein they reside. No

State shall make or enforce any law which shall abridge the privileges or immunities of citizens of the United States; nor shall any State deprive any person of life, liberty, or property, without due process of law; nor deny to any person within its jurisdiction the equal protection of the laws.

Section 2. Representatives shall be apportioned among the several States according to their respective numbers, counting the whole number of persons in each State, excluding Indians not taxed. But when the right to vote at any election for the choice of electors for President and Vice President of the United States, Representatives in Congress, the Executive and Judicial officers of a State, or the members of the Legislature thereof, is denied to any of the male inhabitants of such State, being *twenty-one* years of age, and citizens of the United States, or in any way abridged, except for participation in rebellion, or other crime, the basis of representation therein shall be reduced in the proportion which the number of such male citizens shall bear to the whole number of male citizens twenty-one years of age in such State.

Section 3. No person shall be a Senator or Representative in Congress, or elector of President and Vice President, or hold any office, civil or military, under the United States, or under any State, who, having previously taken an oath, as a member of Congress, or as an officer of the United States, or as a member of any State legislature, or as an executive or judicial officer of any State, to support the Constitution of the United States, shall have engaged in insurrection or rebellion against the same, or given aid or comfort to the enemies thereof. But Congress may by a vote of two-thirds of each House, remove such disability.

Section 4. The validity of the public debt of the United States, authorized by law, including debts incurred for payment of pensions and bounties for services in suppressing insurrection or rebellion, shall not be questioned. But neither the United States nor any State shall assume or pay any debt or obligation incurred in aid of insurrection or rebellion against the United States, or any claim for the loss or emancipation of any slave; but all such debts, obligations and claims shall be held illegal and void.

Section 5. The Congress shall have power to enforce, by appropriate legislation, the provisions of this article.

Amendment XV (1870)

Section 1. The right of citizens of the United States to vote shall not be denied or abridged by the United States or by any State on account of race, color, or previous condition of servitude.

Section 2. The Congress shall have power to enforce this article by appropriate legislation.

Amendment XVI (1913)

The Congress shall have power to lay and collect taxes on incomes, from whatever source derived, without apportionment among the several States, and without regard to any census or enumeration.

Amendment XVII (1913)

The Senate of the United States shall be composed of two Senators from each State, elected by the people thereof, for six years; and each Senator shall have one vote. The electors in each State shall have the qualifications requisite for electors of the most numerous branch of the State legislatures.

When vacancies happen in the representation of any State in the Senate, the executive authority of such State shall issue writs of election to fill such vacancies: Provided, That the legislature of any State may empower the executive thereof to make temporary appointments until the people fill the vacancies by election as the legislature may direct.

This amendment shall not be so construed as to affect the election or term of any Senator chosen before it becomes valid as part of the Constitution.

Amendment XVIII (1919)
Section 1. After one year from the ratification of this article the manufacture, sale, or transportation of intoxicating liquors within, the importation thereof into, or the exportation thereof from the United States and all territory subject to the jurisdiction thereof for beverage purposes is hereby prohibited.

Section 2. The Congress and the several States shall have concurrent power to enforce this article by appropriate legislation.

Section 3. This article shall be inoperative unless it shall have been ratified as an amendment to the Constitution by the legislatures of the several States, as provided in the Constitution, within seven years from the date of the submission hereof to the States by the Congress.

Amendment XIX (1920)
The right of citizens of the United States to vote shall not be

denied or abridged by the United States or by any State on account of sex.

Congress shall have power to enforce this article by appropriate legislation.

Amendment XX (1933)
Section 1. The terms of the President and Vice President shall end at noon on the 20th day of January, and the terms of Senators and Representatives at noon on the 3d day of January, of the years in which such terms would have ended if this article had not been ratified; and the terms of their successors shall then begin.

Section 2. The Congress shall assemble at least once in every year, and such meeting shall begin at noon on the 3d day of January, unless they shall by law appoint a different day.

Section 3. If, at the time fixed for the beginning of the term of the President, the President elect shall have died, the Vice President elect shall become President. If a President shall not have been chosen before the time fixed for the beginning of his term, or if the President elect shall have failed to qualify, then the Vice President elect shall act as President until a President shall have qualified; and the Congress may by law provide for the case wherein neither a President elect nor a Vice President elect shall have qualified, declaring who shall then act as President, or the manner in which one who is to act shall be selected, and such person shall act accordingly until a President or Vice President shall have qualified.

Section 4. The Congress may by law provide for the case

of the death of any of the persons from whom the House of Representatives may choose a President whenever the right of choice shall have devolved upon them, and for the case of the death of any of the persons from whom the Senate may choose a Vice President whenever the right of choice shall have devolved upon them.

Section 5. Sections 1 and 2 shall take effect on the 15th day of October following the ratification of this article.

Section 6. This article shall be inoperative unless it shall have been ratified as an amendment to the Constitution by the legislatures of three-fourths of the several States within seven years from the date of its submission.

Amendment XXI (1933)
Section 1. The eighteenth article of amendment to the Constitution of the United States is hereby repealed.

Section 2. The transportation or importation into any State, Territory, or possession of the United States for delivery or use therein of intoxicating liquors, in violation of the laws thereof, is hereby prohibited.

Section 3. This article shall be inoperative unless it shall have been ratified as an amendment to the Constitution by conventions in the several States, as provided in the Constitution, within seven years from the date of the submission hereof to the States by the Congress.

Amendment XXII (1951)
Section 1. No person shall be elected to the office of the

President more than twice, and no person who has held the office of President, or acted as President, for more than two years of a term to which some other person was elected President shall be elected to the office of the President more than once. But this Article shall not apply to any person holding the office of President, when this Article was proposed by the Congress, and shall not prevent any person who may be holding the office of President, or acting as President, during the term within which this Article becomes operative from holding the office of President or acting as President during the remainder of such term.

Section 2. This article shall be inoperative unless it shall have been ratified as an amendment to the Constitution by the legislatures of three-fourths of the several States within seven years from the date of its submission to the States by the Congress.

Amendment XXIII (1961)
Section 1. The District constituting the seat of Government of the United States shall appoint in such manner as the Congress may direct:

A number of electors of President and Vice President equal to the whole number of Senators and Representatives in Congress to which the District would be entitled if it were a State, but in no event more than the least populous State; they shall be in addition to those appointed by the States, but they shall be considered, for the purposes of the election of President and Vice President, to be electors appointed by a State; and they shall meet in the District and perform such duties as provided by the twelfth article of amendment.

Section 2. The Congress shall have power to enforce this article by appropriate legislation.

Amendment XXIV (1964)

Section 1. The right of citizens of the United States to vote in any primary or other election for President or Vice President for electors for President or Vice President, or for Senator or Representative in Congress, shall not be denied or abridged by the United States or any State by reason of failure to pay any poll tax or other tax.

Section 2. The Congress shall have power to enforce this article by appropriate legislation.

Amendment XXV (1967)

Section 1. In case of the removal of the President from office or of his death or resignation, the Vice President shall become President.

Section 2. Whenever there is a vacancy in the office of the Vice President, the President shall nominate a Vice President who shall take office upon confirmation by a majority vote of both Houses of Congress.

Section 3. Whenever the President transmits to the President pro tempore of the Senate and the Speaker of the House of Representatives his written declaration that he is unable to discharge the powers and duties of his office, and until he transmits to them a written declaration to the contrary, such powers and duties shall be discharged by the Vice President as Acting President.

Section 4. Whenever the Vice President and a majority of either the principal officers of the executive departments or of such other body as Congress may by law provide, transmit to the President pro tempore of the Senate and the Speaker of the House of Representatives their written declaration that the President is unable to discharge the powers and duties of his office, the Vice President shall immediately assume the powers and duties of the office as Acting President.

Thereafter, when the President transmits to the President pro tempore of the Senate and the Speaker of the House of Representatives his written declaration that no inability exists, he shall resume the powers and duties of his office unless the Vice President and a majority of either the principal officers of the executive department or of such other body as Congress may by law provide, transmit within four days to the President pro tempore of the Senate and the Speaker of the House of Representatives their written declaration that the President is unable to discharge the powers and duties of his office. Thereupon Congress shall decide the issue, assembling within forty-eight hours for that purpose if not in session. If the Congress, within twenty-one days after receipt of the latter written declaration, or, if Congress is not in session, within twenty-one days after Congress is required to assemble, determines by two-thirds vote of both Houses that the President is unable to discharge the powers and duties of his office, the Vice President shall continue to discharge the same as Acting President; otherwise, the President shall resume the powers and duties of his office.

Amendment XXVI (1971)

Section 1. The right of citizens of the United States, who are eighteen years of age or older, to vote shall not be denied or abridged by the United States or by any State on account of age.

Section 2. The Congress shall have power to enforce this article by appropriate legislation.

Amendment XXVII (1992)
No law varying the compensation for the services of the Senators and Representatives shall take effect, until an election of Representatives shall have intervened.

PREVIOUS DRAFTS OF THE 22ND AMENDMENT

Jan. 3, 1947
"[no] personal shall be chosen or serve as President of the United States for any term, or be eligible to hold the office of President during any term, if such person shall have heretofore served as President during the whole or any part of each of any two separate terms."

Feb. 5, 1947
"Any person who has served as President of the United States during all, or portions, of any two terms, shall therefore be ineligible to hold the office of President."

Feb. 6, 1947
A person who has held the office of the President, or acted as President, on three hundred and sixty-five calendar days or more in each of two terms *shall not be eligible to hold* the office of the President, or to act as President, for any part of another term.

March 10, 1947
No person shall be elected to the office of President more than twice.

March 12, 1947
No person shall be elected to the office of the President more than twice, and no person who has held the office of president or acted as President for more than 2 years of a term to which some other person was elected President, shall be *elected* to the office of the President more than once.

THE FEDERALIST PAPERS

No. 68: The Mode of Electing the President (March 14, 1788) (Hamilton)

THE mode of appointment of the Chief Magistrate of the United States is almost the only part of the system, of any consequence, which has escaped without severe censure, or which has received the slightest mark of approbation from its opponents. The most plausible of these, who has appeared in print, has even deigned to admit that the election of the President is pretty well guarded. I venture somewhat further, and hesitate not to affirm, that if the manner of it be not perfect, it is at least excellent. It unites in an eminent degree all the advantages, the union of which was to be wished for.

It was desirable that the sense of the people should operate in the choice of the person to whom so important a trust was to be confided. This end will be answered by committing the right of making it, not to any preestablished body, but to men chosen by the people for the special purpose, and at the particular conjuncture.

It was equally desirable, that the immediate election should be made by men most capable of analyzing the qualities adapted to the station, and acting under circumstances favorable to deliberation, and to a judicious combination of all the reasons and inducements which were proper to govern their choice. A small number of persons, selected by their fellow-citizens from the general mass, will be most likely to possess the information and discernment requisite to such complicated investigations.

It was also peculiarly desirable to afford as little opportunity as possible to tumult and disorder. This evil was not least to be dreaded in the election of a magistrate, who was to have so important an agency in the administration of the government as the President of the United States. But the precautions which have been so happily concerted in the system under consideration, promise an effectual security against this mischief. The choice of SEVERAL, to form an intermediate body of electors, will be much less apt to convulse the community with any extraordinary or violent movements, than the choice of ONE who was himself to be the final object of the public wishes. And as the electors, chosen in each State, are to assemble and vote in the State in which they are chosen, this detached and divided situation will expose them much less to heats and ferments, which might be communicated from them to the people, than if they were all to be convened at one time, in one place.

Nothing was more to be desired than that every practicable obstacle should be opposed to cabal, intrigue, and corruption. These most deadly adversaries of republican government might naturally have been expected to make their approaches from more than one querter, but chiefly from the desire in foreign powers to gain an improper ascendant in our councils. How could they better gratify this, than by raising a creature of their own to the chief magistracy of the Union? But the convention have guarded against all danger of this sort, with the most provident and judicious attention. They have not made the appointment of the President to depend on any preexisting bodies of men, who might be tampered with beforehand to prostitute their votes; but they have referred it in the first instance to an immediate act of the people of America, to be exerted in the choice of persons for the temporary and sole purpose of making the appointment. And they have excluded from eligibility to this trust, all those who from situation might be suspected of too great devotion to the President in office. No senator, representative, or other person holding a place of trust or profit under the United States, can be of the numbers of the electors.

Thus without corrupting the body of the people, the immediate agents in the election will at least enter upon the task free from any sinister bias. Their transient existence, and their detached situation, already taken notice of, afford a satisfactory prospect of their continuing so, to the conclusion of it. The business of corruption, when it is to embrace so considerable a number of men, requires time as well as means. Nor would it be found easy suddenly to embark them, dispersed as they would be over thirteen States, in any combinations founded upon motives, which though they could not properly be denominated corrupt, might yet be of a nature to mislead them from their duty.

Another and no less important desideratum was, that the Executive should be independent for his continuance in office on all but the people themselves. He might otherwise be tempted to sacrifice his duty to his complaisance for those whose favor was necessary to the duration of his official consequence. This advantage will also be secured, by making his re-election to depend on a special body of representatives, deputed by the society for the single purpose of making the important choice.

All these advantages will happily combine in the plan devised by the convention; which is, that the people of each State shall choose a number of persons as electors, equal to the number of senators and representatives of such State in the national government, who shall assemble within the State, and vote for some fit person as President. Their votes, thus given, are to be transmitted to the seat of the national government, and the person who may happen to have a majority of the whole number of votes will be the President. But as a majority of the votes might not always happen to centre in one man, and as it might be unsafe to permit less than a majority to be conclusive, it is provided that, in such a contingency, the

House of Representatives shall select out of the candidates who shall have the five highest number of votes, the man who in their opinion may be best qualified for the office.

The process of election affords a moral certainty, that the office of President will never fall to the lot of any man who is not in an eminent degree endowed with the requisite qualifications. Talents for low intrigue, and the little arts of popularity, may alone suffice to elevate a man to the first honors in a single State; but it will require other talents, and a different kind of merit, to establish him in the esteem and confidence of the whole Union, or of so considerable a portion of it as would be necessary to make him a successful candidate for the distinguished office of President of the United States. It will not be too strong to say, that there will be a constant probability of seeing the station filled by characters pre-eminent for ability and virtue. And this will be thought no inconsiderable recommendation of the Constitution, by those who are able to estimate the share which the executive in every government must necessarily have in its good or ill administration. Though we cannot acquiesce in the political heresy of the poet who says: "For forms of government let fools contest That which is best administered is best," yet we may safely pronounce, that the true test of a good government is its aptitude and tendency to produce a good administration.

The Vice-President is to be chosen in the same manner with the President; with this difference, that the Senate is to do, in respect to the former, what is to be done by the House of Representatives, in respect to the latter.

The appointment of an extraordinary person, as Vice-President, has been objected to as superfluous, if not mischievous. It has been alleged, that it would have been preferable to have authorized the Senate to elect out of their own body an officer answering that description. But two considerations seem to justify the ideas of the convention in this respect. One is, that to secure at all times the possibility of a definite resolution of the body, it is necessary that the President should have only a casting vote. And to take the senator of any State from his seat as senator, to place him in that of President of the Senate, would be to exchange, in regard to the State from which he came, a constant for a contingent vote. The other consideration is, that as the Vice-President may occasionally become a substitute for the President, in the supreme executive magistracy, all the reasons which recommend the mode of election prescribed for the one, apply with great if not with equal force to the manner of appointing the other. It is remarkable that in this, as in most other instances, the objection which is made would lie against the constitution of this State. We have a Lieutenant-Governor, chosen by the people at large, who presides in the Senate, and is the constitutional substitute for the Governor, in casualties similar to those which would authorize the Vice-President to exercise the authorities and discharge the duties of the President.

No. 72: The Same Subject Continued, and Re-Eligibility of the Executive Considered
(March 21, 1788) (Hamilton)

THE administration of government, in its largest sense, comprehends all the operations of the body politic, whether legislative, executive, or judiciary; but in its most usual, and perhaps its most precise signification. it is limited to executive details, and falls peculiarly within the province of the executive department. The actual conduct of foreign negotiations, the preparatory plans of finance, the application and disbursement of the public moneys in conformity to the general appropriations of the legislature, the arrangement of the army and navy, the directions of the operations of war, these, and other matters of a like nature, constitute what seems to be most properly understood by the administration of government.

The persons, therefore, to whose immediate management these different matters are committed, ought to be considered as the assistants or deputies of the chief magistrate, and on this account, they ought to derive their offices from his appointment, at least from his nomination, and ought to be subject to his superintendence. This view of the subject will at once suggest to us the intimate connection between the duration of the executive magistrate in office and the stability of the system of administration. To reverse and undo what has been done by a predecessor, is very often considered by a successor as the best proof he can give of his own capacity and desert; and in addition to this propensity, where the alteration has been the result of public choice, the person substituted is warranted in supposing that the dismission of his predecessor has proceeded from a dislike to his measures; and that the less he resembles him, the more he will recommend himself to the favor of his constituents. These considerations, and the influence of personal confidences and attachments, would be likely to induce every new President to promote a change of men to fill the subordinate stations; and these causes together could not fail to occasion a disgraceful and ruinous mutability in the administration of the government.

With a positive duration of considerable extent, I connect the circumstance of re-eligibility. The first is necessary to give to the officer himself the inclination and the resolution to act his part well, and to the community time and leisure to observe the tendency of his measures, and thence to form an experimental estimate of their merits. The last is necessary to enable the people, when they see reason to approve of his conduct, to continue him in his station, in order to prolong the utility of his talents and virtues, and to secure to the government the advantage of permanency in a wise system of administration.

Nothing appears more plausible at first sight, nor more ill-founded upon close inspection, than a scheme which in relation to the present point has had some respectable advocates, I mean that of continuing the chief magistrate in office for a certain time, and then excluding him from it, either for a limited period or forever after. This exclusion, whether temporary or perpetual, would have nearly the same effects, and these effects would be for the most part rather pernicious than salutary.

One ill effect of the exclusion would be a diminution of the inducements to good behavior. There are few men who would not feel much less zeal in the discharge of a duty when they were conscious that the advantages of the station with which it was connected must be relinquished at a determinate period, than when they were permitted to entertain a hope of OBTAINING, by MERITING, a continuance of them. This position will not be disputed so long as it is admitted that the desire of reward is one of the strongest incentives of human conduct; or that the best security for the fidelity of mankind is to make their interests coincide with their duty. Even the love of fame, the ruling passion of the noblest minds, which would prompt a man to plan and undertake extensive and arduous enterprises for the public benefit, requiring considerable time to mature and perfect them, if he could flatter himself with the prospect of being allowed to finish what he had begun, would, on the contrary, deter him from the undertaking, when he foresaw that he must quit the scene before he could accomplish the work, and must commit that, together with his own reputation, to hands which might be unequal or unfriendly to the task. The most to be expected from the generality of men, in such a situation, is the negative merit of not doing harm, instead of the positive merit of doing good.

Another ill effect of the exclusion would be the temptation to sordid views, to peculation, and, in some instances, to usurpation. An avaricious man, who might happen to fill the office, looking forward to a time when he must at all events yield up the emoluments he enjoyed, would feel a propensity, not easy to be resisted by such a man, to make the best use of the opportunity he enjoyed while it lasted, and might not scruple to have recourse to the most corrupt expedients to make the harvest as abundant as it was transitory; though the same man, probably, with a different prospect before him, might content himself with the regular perquisites of his situation, and might even be unwilling to risk the consequences of an abuse of his opportunities. His avarice might be a guard upon his avarice. Add to this that the same man might be vain or ambitious, as well as avaricious. And if he could expect to prolong his honors by his good conduct, he might hesitate to sacrifice his appetite for them to his appetite for gain. But with the prospect before him of approaching an inevitable annihilation, his avarice would be likely to get the victory over his caution, his vanity, or his ambition.

An ambitious man, too, when he found himself seated on the summit of his country's honors, when he looked forward to the time at which he must descend from the exalted eminence for ever, and reflected that no exertion of merit on his part could save him from the unwelcome reverse; such a man, in such a situation, would be much more violently tempted to embrace a favorable conjuncture for attempting the prolongation of his power, at every personal hazard, than if he had the probability of answering the same end by doing his duty.

Would it promote the peace of the community, or the

stability of the government to have half a dozen men who had had credit enough to be raised to the seat of the supreme magistracy, wandering among the people like discontented ghosts, and sighing for a place which they were destined never more to possess?

A third ill effect of the exclusion would be, the depriving the community of the advantage of the experience gained by the chief magistrate in the exercise of his office. That experience is the parent of wisdom, is an adage the truth of which is recognized by the wisest as well as the simplest of mankind. What more desirable or more essential than this quality in the governors of nations? Where more desirable or more essential than in the first magistrate of a nation?

Can it be wise to put this desirable and essential quality under the ban of the Constitution, and to declare that the moment it is acquired, its possessor shall be compelled to abandon the station in which it was acquired, and to which it is adapted? This, nevertheless, is the precise import of all those regulations which exclude men from serving their country, by the choice of their fellow citizens, after they have by a course of service fitted themselves for doing it with a greater degree of utility.

A fourth ill effect of the exclusion would be the banishing men from stations in which, in certain emergencies of the state, their presence might be of the greatest moment to the public interest or safety. There is no nation which has not, at one period or another, experienced an absolute necessity of the services of particular men in particular situations; perhaps it would not be too strong to say, to the preservation of its political existence. How unwise, therefore, must be every such self-denying ordinance as serves to prohibit a nation from making use of its own citizens in the manner best suited to its exigencies and circumstances! Without supposing the personal essentiality of the man, it is evident that a change of the chief magistrate, at the breaking out of a war, or at any similar crisis, for another, even of equal merit, would at all times be detrimental to the community, inasmuch as it would substitute inexperience to experience, and would tend to unhinge and set afloat the already settled train of the administration.

A fifth ill effect of the exclusion would be, that it would operate as a constitutional interdiction of stability in the administration. By NECESSITATING a change of men, in the first office of the nation, it would necessitate a mutability of measures. It is not generally to be expected, that men will vary and measures remain uniform. The contrary is the usual course of things. And we need not be apprehensive that there will be too much stability, while there is even the option of changing; nor need we desire to prohibit the people from continuing their confidence where they think it may be safely placed, and where, by constancy on their part, they may obviate the fatal inconveniences of fluctuating councils and a variable policy.

These are some of the disadvantages which would flow from the principle of exclusion. They apply most forcibly to the scheme of a perpetual exclusion; but when we consider that even a partial exclusion would always render the readmission of the person a remote and precarious object, the observations which have been made will apply nearly as fully to one case as to the other.

What are the advantages promised to counterbalance these disadvantages? They are represented to be: 1st, greater independence in the magistrate; 2d, greater security to the people. Unless the exclusion be perpetual, there will be no pretense to infer the first advantage. But even in that case, may he have no object beyond his present station, to which he may sacrifice his independence? May he have no connections, no friends, for whom he may sacrifice it? May he not be less willing by a firm conduct, to make personal enemies, when he acts under the impression that a time is fast approaching, on the arrival of which he not only MAY, but MUST, be exposed to their resentments, upon an equal, perhaps upon an inferior, footing? It is not an easy point to determine whether his independence would be most promoted or impaired by such an arrangement.

As to the second supposed advantage, there is still greater reason to entertain doubts concerning it. If the exclusion were to be perpetual, a man of irregular ambition, of whom alone there could be reason in any case to entertain apprehension, would, with infinite reluctance, yield to the necessity of taking his leave forever of a post in which his passion for power and pre-eminence had acquired the force of habit. And if he had been fortunate or adroit enough to conciliate the good-will of the people, he might induce them to consider as a very odious and unjustifiable restraint upon themselves, a provision which was calculated to debar them of the right of giving a fresh proof of their attachment to a favorite. There may be conceived circumstances in which this disgust of the people, seconding the thwarted ambition of such a favorite, might occasion greater danger to liberty, than could ever reasonably be dreaded from the possibility of a perpetuation in office, by the voluntary suffrages of the community, exercising a constitutional privilege.

There is an excess of refinement in the idea of disabling the people to continue in office men who had entitled themselves, in their opinion, to approbation and confidence; the advantages of which are at best speculative and equivocal, and are overbalanced by disadvantages far more certain and decisive.

PUBLIUS.

THE PRESIDENTIAL SUCCESSION ACT (1947)

3 U.S. Code § 19 - Vacancy in offices of both President and Vice President; officers eligible to act

(a)

(1) If, by reason of death, resignation, removal from office, inability, or failure to qualify, there is neither a President nor Vice President to discharge the powers and duties of the office of President, then the Speaker of the House of Representatives shall, upon his resignation as Speaker and as Representative in Congress, act as President.

(2) The same rule shall apply in the case of the death, resignation, removal from office, or inability of an individual acting as President under this subsection.

(b)

If, at the time when under subsection (a) of this section a Speaker is to begin the discharge of the powers and duties of the office of President, there is no Speaker, or the Speaker fails to qualify as Acting President, then the President pro tempore of the Senate shall, upon his resignation as President pro tempore and as Senator, act as President.

(c) An individual acting as President under subsection (a) or subsection (b) of this section shall continue to act until the expiration of the then current Presidential term, except that—

(1)
if his discharge of the powers and duties of the office is founded in whole or in part on the failure of both the President-elect and the Vice-President-elect to qualify, then he shall act only until a President or Vice President qualifies; and
(2)
if his discharge of the powers and duties of the office is founded in whole or in part on the inability of the President or Vice President, then he shall act only until the removal of the disability of one of such individuals.

(d)

(1)
If, by reason of death, resignation, removal from office, inability, or failure to qualify, there is no President pro tempore to act as President under subsection (b) of this section, then the officer of the United States who is highest on the following list, and who is not under disability to discharge the powers and duties of the office of President shall act as President: Secretary of State, Secretary of the Treasury, Secretary of Defense, Attorney General, Secretary of the Interior, Secretary of Agriculture, Secretary of Commerce, Secretary of Labor, Secretary of Health and Human Services, Secretary of Housing and Urban Development, Secretary of Transportation, Secretary of Energy, Secretary of Education, Secretary of Veterans Affairs, Secretary of Homeland Security.

(2) An individual acting as President under this subsection shall continue so to do until the expiration of the then current Presidential term, but not after a qualified and prior-entitled individual is able to act, except that the removal of the disability of an individual higher on the list contained in paragraph

(1) of this subsection or the ability to qualify on the part of an individual higher on such list shall not terminate his service.

(3)

The taking of the oath of office by an individual specified in the list in paragraph (1) of this subsection shall be held to constitute his resignation from the office by virtue of the holding of which he qualifies to act as President.

(e)

Subsections (a), (b), and (d) of this section shall apply only to such officers as are eligible to the office of President under the Constitution. Subsection (d) of this section shall apply only to officers appointed, by and with the advice and consent of the Senate, prior to the time of the death, resignation, removal from office, inability, or failure to qualify, of the President pro tempore, and only to officers not under impeachment by the House of Representatives at the time the powers and duties of the office of President devolve upon them.

(f)

During the period that any individual acts as President under this section, his compensation shall be at the rate then provided by law in the case of the President.

(June 25, 1948, ch. 644, 62 Stat. 677; Pub. L. 89–174, § 6(a), Sept. 9, 1965, 79 Stat. 669; Pub. L. 89–670, § 10(a), Oct. 15, 1966, 80 Stat. 948; Pub. L. 91–375, § 6(b), Aug. 12, 1970, 84 Stat. 775; Pub. L. 95–91, title VII, § 709(g), Aug. 4, 1977, 91 Stat. 609; Pub. L. 96–88, title V, § 508(a), Oct. 17, 1979, 93 Stat. 692; Pub. L. 100–527, § 13(a), Oct. 25, 1988, 102 Stat. 2643; Pub. L. 109–177, title V, § 503, Mar. 9, 2006, 120 Stat. 247.)

CURRENT PRESIDENTIAL LINE OF SUCCESSION (2026) AS PER PRESIDENTIAL SUCCESSION ACT

No.	Office	Incumbent	Party
1	Vice President	JD Vance	Republican
2	Speaker of the House of Representatives	Mike Johnson	Republican
3	President pro tempore of the Senate	Chuck Grassley	Republican
4	Secretary of State	Marco Rubio	Republican
5	Secretary of the Treasury	Scott Bessent	Republican
6	Secretary of Defense	Pete Hegseth	Republican
7	Attorney General	Pam Bondi	Republican
8	Secretary of the Interior	Doug Burgum	Republican
9	Secretary of Agriculture	Brooke Rollins	Republican
10	Secretary of Commerce	Howard Lutnick	Republican
11	Secretary of Labor	Lori Chavez-DeRemer	Republican
12	Secretary of Health and Human Services	Robert F. Kennedy Jr.	Independent
13	Secretary of Housing and Urban Development	Scott Turner	Republican
14	Secretary of Transportation	Sean Duffy	Republican
15	Secretary of Energy	Chris Wright	Republican
16	Secretary of Education	Linda McMahon	Republican
17	Secretary of Veterans Affairs	Doug Collins	Republican
18	Secretary of Homeland Security	Kristi Noem	Republican

PRESIDENTIAL SUCCESSION BY VICE PRESIDENTS

Successor	Party	President	Reason	Date of Succession
John Tyler	Whig	William Henry Harrison	Death	April 1, 1841 (31 days into Harrison's presidency)
Millard Fillmore	Whig	Zachary Taylor	Death	July 9, 1850 (1 year, 4 months, 5 days into Taylor's presidency)
Andrew Johnson	National Union (Democratic)	Abraham Lincoln	Assassination	April 15, 1865 (1 month, 11 days into Lincoln's second term)
Chester A. Arthur	Republican	James A. Garfield	Assassination	September 19, 1881 (6 months, 15 days into Garfield's presidency)
Theodore Roosevelt	Republican	William McKinley	Assassination	September 14, 1901 (6 months, 10 days into McKinley's second term)

Successor	Party	President	Reason	Date of Succession
Calvin Coolidge	Republican	Warren G. Harding	Death	August 2, 1923 (2 years, 5 months, 29 days into Harding's presidency)
Harry S. Truman	Democratic	Franklin D. Roosevelt	Death	April 12, 1945 (3 months, 23 days into Roosevelt's fourth term)
Lyndon B. Johnson	Democratic	John F. Kennedy	Assassination	November 22, 1963 (2 years, 10 months, 2 days into Kennedy's presidency)
Gerald Ford	Republican	Richard Nixon	Resignation	August 9, 1974 (1 year, 6 months, 20 days into Nixon's sec-ond term)

ACTING PRESIDENTS UNDER THE 25TH AMENDMENT

Date	President Temporarily Transferring Power	Acting President	Reason for Temporary Transfer of Power
July 13, 1985	Ronald Reagan	George H. W. Bush	Underwent surgery to remove cancerous polyps from colon (general anesthesia).
June 29, 2002	George W. Bush	Dick Cheney	Underwent routine colonoscopy (sedation).
July 21, 2007	George W. Bush	Dick Cheney	Underwent routine colonoscopy (sedation).
November 19, 2021	Joe Biden	Kamala Harris	Underwent routine colonoscopy (sedation).

Index

★ ★ ★